"What better place is there to be, except at the feet of Jesus! Scott uses his own life experiences to help others and tries to motivate us to think about our faith. The words are written in plain English and would be easily understood by a new believer with plenty of new insights for older ones." —E.B.

"Scott Brooks offers refreshingly simple insights into having a friendship with God." —A.R.

"There are many people in the world looking for answers to why they are here and how to get to know God. I believe that a lot of these questions have been answered in AT HIS FEET." —G.B.

"His practical ideas and analogies deliver a belief that consistent closeness to the Lord is achievable." —G.W.

"Scott gives practical advice on how to grow closer in relationship with the Holy One. I know that I will read it again and learn more each time I do. —M.E.

"I feel that this book successfully shows the elements of God's character and provides a way to achieve an honest relationship with Him. —J.B.

"Scott's book is written from the heart as a traveler showing others the landmarks along the way. His book combines observations from life, theological perception, insights from the Bible and, most of all, practical tips for beginning to live life at Jesus' feet. —W.F.B.

"Many times, new Christians are left on their own to discover what a relationship with Christ looks and feels like. AT HIS FEET is a must read for individuals new to the faith and those who are looking to go deeper in their walk with Christ. It will bring you closer to Christ and put you at the exact place we should all be—at His feet." —R.M.

"AT HIS FEET gives ideas to help us grow in our spiritual lives and causes us to pause and think about our lives, and what really are our priorities in life." —R.C.

"I really enjoyed AT HIS FEET! There were many parts that hit home to me. For one thing, it helped me to see Jesus in a more human light and think of Him as a friend. I think AT HIS FEET will be a great read for people who have just accepted the Lord as their Savior and also for those who have already been walking in the Light but need a "refresher" on some things. —S.B.

At His Feet

Scott Brooks

At His Feet
by Scott Brooks
Copyright ©2005 Scott Brooks

All rights reserved. This book is protected under the copyright laws of the United States of America. This book may not be copied or reprinted for commercial gain or profit. The use of short quotations or occasional page copying for personal or group study is permitted and encouraged. Permission will be granted upon request. Unless otherwise identified, Scripture quotations are from the New Living Translation, copyright ©1996. Used by permission of Tyndale House Publishers, Inc., Wheaton, Illinois 60189. All rights reserved.

ISBN 1-58169-172-6
For Worldwide Distribution
Printed in the U.S.A.

Gazelle Press
P.O. Box 191540 • Mobile, AL 36619
800-367-8203

Table of Contents

Introduction		ix
Chapter 1	Having Soft and Teachable Hearts	1
Chapter 2	The Value and Privilege of Learning From God	24
Chapter 3	Practical Ways to Learn From God	36
Chapter 4	Friendship With God	53
Chapter 5	A Priority of Time	97
Chapter 6	Summary	110
Appendix		112

Dedication

I dedicate this book to the One to whom
I owe my very existence...
the One at whose feet I love to sit.

Introduction

The Bible speaks of a woman named Martha who invited Jesus into her home. While Martha was busy with preparations for the meal, her sister, Mary, sat at Jesus' feet, spending time with Him and learning from Him. As Martha became more and more stressed and uptight because of the cooking and housework, she became upset that Mary wasn't helping with the preparations. Finally, Martha interrupted her sister's time with the Lord. Martha told Jesus that she didn't think it was fair that she was doing all of the work, and then she asked Jesus to tell Mary to help her. Jesus kindly responded by telling her that while she was worried and upset about many things, Mary had discovered what was better and that her time with Him would not be taken from her. (See Luke 10:38-42.)

I love this passage of the Bible. When I picture Mary sitting at the feet of Jesus, the Lord of the universe, learning from Him and growing in her friendship with Him, it stirs something warm in my heart, and I desire to live my life from that same place—at the feet of my Lord. I think, *Wow, what a privilege to be with Jesus, to learn from Him, and to grow in friendship with Him!* He is the best Friend I could ever have—the One who is perfect in character and cares for me completely. I can think of no higher privilege than to live life from this place—at Jesus' feet!

During the times I've lived at Jesus' feet, I've seen God

bring forth good things through His Holy Spirit within me, including the fruit of the Spirit: "love, joy, peace, patience, kindness, goodness, faithfulness, gentleness and self-control" (Galatians 5:22-23). In turn, these "good things" have positively affected my relationship with God and my relationships with my family, friends, and other people.

Contained within the pages of this book are practical ideas and suggestions that can help both you and me to grow in living at Jesus' feet. I am incomplete in my understanding of all that is needed to do this well, but in this book I share those things that I have found to be helpful in my life. I have a strong desire to keep these things in focus, for I know if I lose sight of them, then I will miss what is most important in life—those things that are God's best for me.

In one of my past summer jobs, I had a boss whom I really appreciated. My boss did not make any assumptions as to what I knew or didn't know. Instead, he shared with me all the details that I might need to do my job well. Some of these things I already knew, but there were some things of which I wasn't aware. I was very thankful that he shared every detail with me so that I could see what I was missing and in what areas I needed to grow.

In a similar way, I will include in this book many details about what is needed to live our lives well at Jesus' feet. If you have already been in relationship with God for a long time, my desire is that God would bring these details to life inside of you and refresh your perspective on those things that are critical to your life with Him. On the other hand, if you are brand new in your relationship with God, my desire is that God would bring these details to life in your heart and cause them to be of great value to you throughout your life with Him. If you have never read the Bible, I hope the many Scripture passages included in this book will provide you with an exciting introduction to the riches of God's Word. The Bible is a powerful tool that God can use in all of our hearts and lives.

The content in this book is very valuable to me, and I always want to keep it as the focus of my life. One of the reasons I am writing this book is so that I can periodically read it every year or two in order to focus and refocus upon these important things. I'm also writing this book for you, and I welcome you to join me in keeping these important things in view. My desire is that both you and I would grow and blossom into what is God's best for us, as we live our lives at this very privileged place-at His feet.

Every time I read this book, I plan to ask God to soften my heart and cause things to stand out to me. This way, each time I read it, God will illuminate the things that are most relevant to my life at that time. I welcome you to join me in asking God for the same thing—a softened heart and His illumination of the things most pertinent to your life. Hopefully you will not just read what I have written, but you will also hear what God wants to speak to you through this book. I truly hope that you find this book to be of great value in your life, that you are encouraged at how God uses it in your life, and that it will be an encouragement for you to continue to live your life well *at Jesus' feet.*

—Scott Brooks, 2005

Chapter 1

Having Soft and Teachable Hearts

There was once a man who had such a bad heart condition that it eventually killed him. But his condition wasn't an issue of the hardening of his arteries or any other disease in his heart—it was his spiritual heart that had hardened. Because of this condition, the man made all sorts of poor decisions in his life. Unfortunately, this man was a man of influence, and due to his poor decisions, terrible destruction came to the country he ruled, including the deaths of many people and the loss of his own life, as well.

If you have not guessed it already, I'm writing about Pharaoh, the ruler of Egypt at the time of Moses, the man who hardened his heart against God over and over again.

In stark contrast to Pharaoh's attitude toward God, we

have the picture of Mary, the sister of Martha, humbly sitting at Jesus' feet. Mary had a soft, teachable heart, as opposed to Pharaoh's arrogant one.

In this chapter, we'll take a look at this very important issue of our spiritual heart condition. We'll examine our spiritual hearts, as well as explore some of the keys to having "good" hearts before God, so that, like Mary, we can also blossom at the feet of Jesus.

What Do Our Hearts Look Like?

Jesus once told a parable that explains what our spiritual hearts are like. In the story, a farmer sowed seed, which fell on various types of ground: Some fell on the footpath, some fell on shallow soil, some on thorny ground, and still others in fertile soil. The seed only grew well in the fertile soil, where it produced a bountiful harvest. When His disciples asked Him the following question, Jesus' answer reveals much about the human heart.

> *His disciples came and asked him, "Why do you always tell stories when you talk to the people?" Then he explained to them, "You have been permitted to understand the secrets of the Kingdom of Heaven, but others have not. To those who are open to my teaching, more understanding will be given, and they will have an abundance of knowledge. But to those who are not listening, even what they have*

Having Soft and Teachable Hearts

will be taken away from them. That is why I tell these stories, because people see what I do, but they don't really see. They hear what I say, but they don't really hear, and they don't understand. This fulfills the prophecy of Isaiah, which says:

'You will hear my words, but you will not understand; you will see what I do, but you will not perceive its meaning. For the hearts of these people are hardened, and their ears cannot hear, and they have closed their eyes—so their eyes cannot see, and their ears cannot hear, and their hearts cannot understand, and they cannot turn to me and let me heal them.'

But blessed are your eyes, because they see; and your ears, because they hear. I assure you, many prophets and godly people have longed to see and hear what you have seen and heard, but they could not (Matthew 13:10-17).

Jesus then went on to explain the meaning of the parable to His disciples. Jesus is the farmer, and the seed is the word He sows. The various types of ground represented the various types of people's hearts that hear His word. Different hearts receive His word in different ways, and there are many things that can hinder us from having good "heart soil" before God. We face many temptations that can hinder us from growing, just as the seeds faced adverse conditions when they fell on the thorny ground. If our hearts become hard like the footpath soil, they will be poor receptors of His word, and we won't learn well at Jesus' feet. But if we have responsive hearts before God and receive His word as the fertile soil received the seed, we will grow and be fruitful in those things that are God's best for us.

There is another Bible passage that provides us with a helpful key as to how we can have good heart soil.

> *Great crowds were following Jesus. He turned around and said to them, "If you want to be my follower you must love me more than your own father and mother, wife and children, brothers and sisters-yes, more than your own life. Otherwise, you cannot be my disciple. And you cannot be my disciple if you do not carry your own cross and follow me. But don't begin until you count the cost. For who would begin construction of a building without first getting estimates and then checking to see if there is enough money to pay the bills? Otherwise, you might complete only the foundation before running out of funds. And then how everyone would laugh at you! They would say, "There's the person who started that building and ran out of money before it was finished!"*

Having Soft and Teachable Hearts

Or what king would ever dream of going to war without first sitting down with his counselors and discussing whether his army of ten thousand is strong enough to defeat the twenty thousand soldiers who are marching against him? If he is not able, then while the enemy is still far away, he will send a delegation to discuss terms of peace. So no one can become my disciple without giving up everything for me. Salt is good for seasoning. But if it loses its flavor, how do you make it salty again? Flavorless salt is good neither for the soil nor for fertilizer. It is thrown away. Anyone who is willing to hear should listen and understand!
(Luke 14:25-35)

At times I have found this passage of Scripture to be very challenging. People who are reading this passage for the first time might even wonder if Jesus were setting an unrealistically high standard, or at least they might think that these instructions would infringe too much on their lives. But the more I learn, the more I realize that this is actually a wonderful passage, one that provides tremendous freedom for all of us. It contains an important key to creating fertile soil within our hearts. You may wonder how I would reach such a conclusion; part of the answer comes out of this simple question: "Who is smarter, God or me?" Obviously, the answer is that God (and likewise, Jesus) is much smarter than I am, much more than I can even begin to fathom. So, if Jesus has made each of the following statements, did He really know what He was saying? Of course, He did!

> *If you want to be My follower, you must love Me more than you love your own father or mother, wife or children, brothers or sisters—yes, even more than your own life. Otherwise, you cannot be My disciple.*
>
> *And you cannot be My disciple if you do not carry your own cross and follow me.*
>
> *No one can become My disciple without giving up everything for Me.*

I find that if I first commit myself to God and trust in His infinite wisdom, over time as I begin to see Him working in my life, I will eventually learn what He already knew all along. In the Parable of the Sower, the seeds had difficulty growing in different soil conditions. Fortunately, God already knows the very best ways to keep our hearts fertile, as good soil, which produces a harvest of fruit.

Consider this analogy: Imagine that God is an expert instructor in music, particularly in teaching the guitar. I decide that I want to learn to play the guitar, but I also decide that I want to do it my own way and not pay attention to His instructions. Deep down I really feel that His instruction is not all that important. With this mindset, should I be surprised at how slowly I progress? But if I have the humility to realize that He is the Master Instructor, and if I am able to wholeheartedly give myself to Him and accept His teaching, then He truly can make me into an accomplished guitarist.

In my own life, there have been numerous occasions in which I hit a spiritual "wall." When I finally looked to God, He helped me realize that I didn't know as much as I thought I did, and He had much better ways for me to get to excellent places. A great example of this occurred when I was still an atheist, but near the point of entering into a relationship with God. I had tried numerous philosophies and other attempts at happiness, but no matter how hard I tried, my desires would still conflict with each other. I couldn't get my desires to mesh with each other toward a common goal. I was tired of trying to find happiness over and over again, and still winding up empty. When I finally came to the decision to enter into a relationship with God, I concluded that I had diligently tried everything else unsuccessfully. I decided that I had nothing else to lose—I would give my life to God to see what He could do with it. It was then that I started to learn that He is more than capable of bringing good things into my life.

My life is a lot like strands of rope that get knotted into a ball, and the more I work at the knots the worse they get. Fortunately I can give the knotted ball to Jesus, and I'm glad that He is willing to untangle the knots and free my life for His purposes. As I continue to daily commit my life to God, I see Him changing my heart into good soil and causing me to grow in fruitful ways as He frees me from snares, temptations, and lures. He also waters me with His love, and I see Him causing me to grow in understanding and character. It is wonderful to see this affect my entire life, including my relationships with my wife and children. This all confirms His plan to me and helps me to know, deep down, that He indeed does know what He is doing, and His path is truly the best path for me to take-even if it is challenging at times.

As I said earlier, it sometimes takes time to see what God is doing in our lives. If our focus is, "I've given my life to God; now what am I going to get out of the deal?" and we are only concerned with short-term gain (although it may not truly be gain), then it would be all too easy to find ourselves among the thorns, or worse.

> *But like young plants in such soil, their roots don't go very deep. At first they get along fine, but they wilt as soon as they have problems or are persecuted because they believe the word. The thorny ground represents those who hear and accept the Good News, but all too quickly the message is crowded out by the cares of this life and the lure of wealth, so no crop is produced* (Matthew 13:21-22).

Jesus has said that we cannot be His disciples unless we carry our crosses and follow Him. He has also said

Having Soft and Teachable Hearts

that no one can be His disciple unless they give up everything for Him. Fortunately, these statements can bring great freedom for us, for as we give our lives fully to Him, He can then bring us to good places in the long run. As Jesus said in John 8:36, "If the Son [Jesus] sets you free, you will indeed be free."

The following story from the Bible gives us a great example of this process. It shows us if we will pick up our crosses and tag along with God in His best for us, God knows exactly what He is doing and will even surprise us at times at what He can wonderfully bring about in our lives.

God had promised Abraham that he and his wife, Sarah, would bear a child even though they were both very old, and Sarah was well past her childbearing years. God also promised that Abraham would have many blessed offspring through this child. Things worked out just as God had promised: Sarah miraculously became pregnant and gave birth to a son, whom they named Isaac. Abraham knew that Isaac was the key to God's promise that he would be the father of many nations.

Abraham was given a test by the Lord, a test that at first seemed to be too difficult to imagine: God asked him to sacrifice his beloved son Isaac, the son of God's promise. Although Abraham struggled with this test, he eventually found the courage to follow through with what God challenged him to do. Because of Abraham's obedience, the Lord provided a ram to take Isaac's place on the altar of sacrifice, and Abraham received this word of promise:

> *This is what the Lord says: Because you have obeyed me and have not withheld even your beloved son, I swear by my own self that I will bless you richly. I will multiply your descendants into countless millions, like the stars of the sky and the sand on the seashore. They will conquer their enemies, and through your descendants, all the nations of the earth will be blessed-all because you have obeyed me* (Genesis 22:16-18).

Abraham was challenged by what God asked him to do, just as we are challenged when Jesus asks us to pick up our crosses and follow Him every day. But Abraham found the courage to follow through with what God challenged him to do, and because of this, he was given a beautiful freedom.

Although it is not explicitly stated in the text, in his heart, it is likely that Abraham took hold of Isaac in unhealthy ways. This, in turn, hindered Abraham from being good soil before God and becoming all that God knew he could become. God's challenge to Abraham helped him to have the freedom of which Jesus would speak centuries later:

> *Jesus said, "If you want to be my follower you*

must love me more than your own father and mother, wife and children, brothers and sisters-yes, more than your own life. Otherwise, you cannot be my disciple" (Luke 14:26).

By being obedient to God's command to sacrifice his son, Abraham essentially gave Isaac back over to God and was freed in his heart of an unhealthy bond. Isaac was then God's first, not Abraham's first, and Abraham was freed to be an excellent father, a steward of his son through God's help. Abraham's heart was freed to first have a primary relationship with God, which would then affect all of his other relationships. As long as Isaac held the primary place in his heart, it was hindering this freedom. It wasn't that God wanted to take Isaac from Abraham, but he wanted to free Abraham from trying to carry what is best carried by God.

Dealing with Fears

It can be a scary thing to come before God and wholeheartedly put the entirety of our lives on His altar, including all of our relationships, our desires, our goals, and even our personalities. And yet, if we look at many examples in the Bible, we find that when people go through this process, God frees them to grow in love, joy, peace, and all of the other good things He has for them. If we are afraid, and if we hold back areas of our lives from God, it might seem like a good idea in the short run, but it will ultimately hinder the tremendous growth process that God wants to bring about in our lives.

As a child, if I had a splinter in my hand, I would go to my mom or dad for help. It was a bit frightening to put my hand in theirs and allow them to work with the tweezers to remove the splinter. But the only way that the splinter could be removed and that my hand could heal to fully function as it was intended to, would be for me to have enough courage to hold my hand steadily in theirs. My parents knew that I might experience some pain in the process, but they were willing to allow this minor pain and discomfort to take place because they knew it was what I needed. In a similar way, God isn't interested in ruining our fun or taking things that we like away from us. Instead, He knows the entire process of our lives, and He knows exactly what is needed to get us to where we can function fully as we were designed to function, even if it requires some suffering on our part or some changes in our lives.

The process of the altar brings us to the place in which we give our entire lives to God, allowing Him to sacrifice those things that hinder us from growing in Him. In turn, He enhances those aspects of our character that are already good. So if we give the entirety of our lives to Him—including what we do with our time, what we do with our energy, our decisions as to where we will go or what we will do—then God can direct us into good things in our lives. But the most important requirement is our willingness to place ourselves entirely in God's hands.

Many of us still experience trepidation when it comes to surrendering all of our lives to God. Is there anything else that can help us deal with our fears, so that we can fully place ourselves in God's hands? In my own life, I have found that an understanding of God's desires and characteristics can help us with our fears of surrender.

Some of God's desires

- He desires our best (Jeremiah 29:11).
- He desires a close relationship with us (John 15:15; Matthew 23:37).
- He desires for us to value ourselves, others, and God (Matthew 22:34-40).
- He desires that we would know that we are significant, both at the present time and throughout eternity (John 13:1-5; Isaiah 49:15-16; Revelation 2:17; 3:12).
- He desires that we would be set free into His very best for our lives (John 8:36; 10:10).

Some of God's characteristics

It is easy to attribute human motives and characteristics to God. But there will always be an "Other-ness" to God—aspects of His character that no human could ever attain. Here is a list of such characteristics:

- He always wants our best (Romans 8:28).
- He is always perfect in His motives (Isaiah 55:8-9).
- He infinitely values us (1 Peter 1:18-19; Romans 5:6-11).
- He is never partial (Romans 2:11; 1 Peter 1:17).
- He never commits injustice (2 Chronicles 19:7).
- He never lies (Numbers 23:19; John 14:6).
- He always has selfless love toward us (1 John 4:8; Jeremiah 31:3; Psalm 36:5-7).
- He is infinitely knowledgeable and wise (Romans 11:33-36; Isaiah 40:28).
- He knows us completely (Matthew 10:30; Psalm 139:1-18).
- He never makes a mistake (2 Samuel 22:31; Deuteronomy 32:4).
- His character and desires have always been and will always be consistent throughout eternity (Hebrews 13:8).

These lists have been derived from many Bible verses. I have also found them to be consistent with my own personal experience with God and what I have experienced of reality.

Side Note: *If you would like to learn more about these desires and characteristics of God, the verses in the parentheses should give you a good place to start.*

If we take time to ponder each of God's desires and characteristics, we will begin to realize how very fortunate we are to have such a wonderful Being to whom we can entrust our lives. It's amazing to realize that He loves and values us intimately, that He knows us completely, that He always wants our best, and that He never makes a mistake. It's also comforting to know that because God wants our best, He will not take us through anything or have us change in any way that would not be good for us. God will never use acceptance or rejection to try to control us. He always loves us, even when we do wrong, and in this love, He helps us to turn from our sins, receive forgiveness through His redeeming work on the cross, and then move on toward what is best for our lives.

There is value in knowing God's desires and character. Trusting in His character is a lot like trusting in an excellent surgeon. If I needed a difficult surgery, I would most likely ask around to find a specialist in that field who had a great reputation. If many people spoke highly of a particular surgeon and attested to the excellent results they had experienced, my confidence in that surgeon would naturally grow, and I would feel more comfortable entrusting my case to him. In a similar way, God's working in the lives of others demonstrates His perfect character. When I read the Bible and see how God has worked in other people's lives, I am encouraged to trust my own life to Him even more. And when other people share with me what God has done in their lives, it inspires me to give my life fully to Him for Him to work out what is best for me.

Taking small steps to trust in God—and in His desires

and character—leads to the ability to then take larger steps. If there were a rickety bridge that spanned a raging river, we might "trust" in that bridge all we wanted, but we might still find that if we step out on it, we could fall through and be swept away. But if there were a well-built, solid bridge over that same raging river, then we might still be fearful, but as we step onto the bridge, we find that it truly holds our weight. The more steps we take, the more we realize the solidness of the bridge and our overall confidence increases. In this process, our first steps might be easier if we knew the bridge's architect and his/her excellent reputation in building only solid, high-tolerance bridges.

At one point in his life, Jacob stepped out onto the bridge of trust in God, but only after he had first struck a deal with the Lord:

> *Then Jacob made this vow: "If God will be with me and protect me on this journey and give me food and clothing, and if he will bring me back safely to my father, **then I will make the LORD my God**"* (Genesis 28:20-21, emphasis mine).

I think it is interesting that God didn't say, "Hey, Jacob, I said to pick up your cross and follow Me fully! Why are you challenging what I said?" Instead, God honored Jacob's request. The text seems to imply that Jacob truly wanted to follow God's best for him, but at the same time, he knew there were things that frightened him. So rather than going forward and becoming more fearful about these things, he instead decided to make a deal with God. Jacob essentially told God that if He would help him with his fears, then he would gladly follow God. God agreed to this deal; not only did He help Jacob to overcome his fears, but He also helped Jacob to pick up his cross and follow after Him. What about us? Would making a deal with God help us with any fear we might have of taking up our own crosses and following the Lord?

There are many other Bible verses that show how God can help us with our fears as we share our concerns with Him.

> *Give all your worries and cares to God, for he cares about what happens to you* (1 Peter 5:7).

> *Don't worry about anything; instead, pray about everything. Tell God what you need, and thank him for all he has done. If you do this, you will experience God's peace, which is far more wonderful than the human mind can understand. His peace will guard your hearts and minds as you live in Christ Jesus* (Philippians 4:6-7)

Relationship Is the Key

As we come to the altar and pick up our cross, it can

seem very challenging at times. We really need God's enabling and help throughout the whole process. Instead of our accomplishing God's best for us, we actually need God to accomplish it through us. If we think we can do it on our own, we will eventually learn the hard reality that we can't—and that is a difficult lesson to learn. God does not want us to run ahead and do things on our own, but instead walk beside Him, building our relationship and friendship with Him in the process. It's a positive relationship growth cycle: As we live our lives with God, in a growing friendship with Him, we'll be able to receive God's love and draw upon His enabling and provision in an even greater way. God will then use this to deepen and develop our relationship with Him!

Two Sides of the Same Coin

There is a question that is commonly asked by people who are new in their relationship with God:

"I committed my life to God and received His finished work on the cross so that I could be forgiven and enter into a relationship with Him. And I thought it was only through this completed work of Jesus on the cross that I am in relationship with God and will go to heaven someday. Yet in this chapter, you seem to imply that we can't be in relationship with God (and eventually enter heaven) unless we pick up our cross and follow Jesus daily. Are these contradictory concepts, or do they work together somehow?"

Having Soft and Teachable Hearts

What we are actually looking at are two sides of the same coin. On one side of the coin, we are not worthy to be God's disciples, and we will not make it to heaven unless, by His grace and enabling, we:

- Daily pick up our cross and follow Him (Luke 14:27).
- Wholeheartedly follow God's best for us (Romans 6:17).
- Refuse to forsake our first love of God (Revelation 2:4-7).
- Overcome any temptations that try to keep us from God's best for us (Revelation 3:4-6).
- Prove ourselves faithful to God (1 Corinthians 4:2).

Side Note: *I have listed the Scripture references in the parentheses above in case you were interested in reading in the Bible where these concepts are explicitly discussed.*

On the other side of the coin is Jesus' payment for us on the cross and His conquest of death by His resurrection. Only because of Jesus' payment for our sins are we made acceptable before God. We do not deserve this at all, but because we have received God's amazing gift of love, we are adopted into God's family and become heirs of His promises. Without Jesus' work on our behalf, none of us would ever be good enough to enter into a relationship with God or to go to heaven. Also on this side of the coin are God's promises for our own lives. As we daily commit our lives to Him and wholeheartedly follow Him in His best for us, He is faithful to bring about good things in our lives and eventually bring us to heaven.

Peter wrote about both sides of the coin in the following passage:

> *As we know Jesus better, his divine power gives us everything we need for living a godly life. He has called us to receive his own glory and goodness! And by that same mighty power, he has given us all of his rich and wonderful promises. He has promised that you will escape the decadence all around you caused by evil desires and that you will share in his divine nature. So make every effort to apply the benefits of these promises to your life. Then your faith will produce a life of moral excellence. A life of moral excellence leads to knowing God better.*
>
> *Knowing God leads to self-control. Self-control leads to patient endurance, and patient endurance leads to godliness. Godliness leads to love for other Christians, and finally you will grow to have genuine love for everyone. The more you grow like this, the more you will become productive and useful in your knowledge of our Lord Jesus Christ. But those who fail to develop these virtues are blind or, at least, very shortsighted. They have already forgotten that God has cleansed them from*

their old life of sin. So, dear brothers and sisters, work hard to prove that you really are among those God has called and chosen. Doing this, you will never stumble or fall away. And God will open wide the gates of heaven for you to enter into the eternal Kingdom of our Lord and Savior Jesus Christ (2 Peter 1:3-11).

Summary

In this chapter we have explored some of the keys needed for us to have soft, teachable hearts that learn from Jesus as Mary did. The rest of this book builds upon these keys. One key is that we wholeheartedly pick up our cross and follow Jesus. Another key is that we lay down our lives on God's altar. But the greatest key is that we focus on our relationship with God and look to Him to accomplish all of this through us, as He draws us near to Him in our hearts. This might seem frightening at first, but understanding God's good desires and His characteristics that work for our freedom and for our very best, is key to our being able to trust Him in this excellent process.

I'd like to end this chapter with two passages from Scripture that are meaningful to me. These passages tie many of this chapter's concepts together. As you read, please notice the words that I have highlighted for further emphasis and then bring these verses before God and ask Him to show you the meaning He has for them in your life.

> *Jesus said, "If you try to keep your life for yourself, you will lose it. But if you give up your life for me, **you will find true life**"* (Matthew 16:25 emphasis mine).

> *Jesus said, "I am the true vine, and my Father is the gardener. He cuts off every branch that doesn't produce fruit, and he prunes the branches that do bear fruit **so they will produce even more**. You have already been pruned for greater fruitfulness by the message I have given you. Remain in me, and I will remain in you. For a branch cannot produce fruit if it is severed from the vine, and you cannot be fruitful apart from me. Yes, I am the vine; you are the branches. **Those who remain in me, and I in them, will produce much fruit. For apart from me you can do nothing**. Anyone who parts from me is thrown away like a useless branch and withers. Such branches are gathered into a pile to be burned. **But if you stay joined to me and my words remain in you**, you may ask any request you like, and it will be granted!*

> ***My true disciples produce much fruit**. This brings great glory to my Father. I have loved you even as the Father has loved me. **Remain***

in my love. When you obey me, you remain in my love, just as I obey my Father and remain in his love. I have told you this so that you will be filled with my joy. Yes, your joy will overflow! I command you to love each other in the same way that I love you.

And here is how to measure it—the greatest love is shown when people lay down their lives for their friends. You are my friends if you obey me. I no longer call you servants, because a master doesn't confide in his servants. Now **you are my friends***, since I have told you everything the Father told me. You didn't choose me. I chose you. I appointed you to go and* **produce fruit that will last***, so that the Father will give you whatever you ask for, using my name. I command you to love each other"* (John 15:1-17).

Chapter 2

The Value and Privilege of Learning From God

Can you imagine what it was like for Mary to sit at the feet of Jesus? Can you imagine what it was like to be able to directly gaze into Jesus' eyes of love, to listen to the love in His voice, to feel so highly valued and cared for by Him who is the God of the universe?

If I had been there at that time, I would have loved to have gone over and sat next to Mary. It would have been such a privilege just to be in Jesus' presence, let alone be able to learn from Him. And if at some point Jesus decided to give out hugs, I would have jumped up to join the line! I also would have enjoyed watching each person smile as Jesus' love abundantly flowed out to them like a river of water.

But here we are in the present day, long after Jesus was resurrected, and He is no longer physically with us like He was with Mary. So, how can we learn from Jesus as Mary did?

In the last chapter, we partially answered that question by discussing a number of prerequisites that are needed if we are to learn from God, such as having a soft and teachable heart, laying down our lives on His altar, realizing that His wisdom is greater than our own, and paying attention to Him as our expert instructor.

In the next chapter we'll answer that question more fully, but for now let's first consider why it is of such value and privilege for us to learn from God.

The Value of Learning from God

It is definitely important for each of us to learn from God. For one reason, it brings great freedom to our lives. It is a lot like learning to read: If we don't know how to read, we will be greatly hindered in life. The list of benefits that literacy brings is practically endless: being able to do your job, learning well in school, reading street signs, even following instructions for putting something together! Without the ability to read, we would need to rely on someone else to read for us in many situations. But if we learn to read for ourselves, we are so much farther along than even if someone were always around to help us. In a similar way, if each of us learns from God, we will bear fruit as the individuals He has designed us to be.

Learning from God ourselves is the key to an important issue I like to call ownership. By "ownership," I mean that it is good for each of us to take personal responsibility to learn from God ourselves. We can certainly benefit from what others have learned from God and are willing to share with us (in much the same way as we benefit from someone else reading for us), but if we only listen to others and do not learn from God ourselves, then we will be greatly disadvantaged and hindered in our growth.

Taking ownership and learning from God ourselves is a lot like driving to a new destination in a car. If we are the one driving, we usually have a much better chance remembering the route than if we are a passenger. It is also like participating in a sporting event or a concert. We can know a lot about a certain sports team or about those playing the instruments at a concert, but we experience a much higher level of ownership if we ourselves are the one playing. It can also be compared to taking a class. It is one thing to memorize the material and to parrot the answers back at test time. But we experience a much higher level of ownership if we have a working knowledge of the material and are able to answer intelligently out of our experience. Taking ownership and learning from God directly is of critical importance to our growing more fruitful in His very best for us. We can see this demonstrated in the following parable:

> Jesus said, "The Kingdom of Heaven can be il-

The Value and Privilege of Learning From God

lustrated by the story of ten bridesmaids who took their lamps and went to meet the bridegroom. Five of them were foolish, and five were wise. The five who were foolish took no oil for their lamps, but the other five were wise enough to take along extra oil. When the bridegroom was delayed, they all lay down and slept. At midnight they were roused by the shout, `Look, the bridegroom is coming! Come out and welcome him!'

"All the bridesmaids got up and prepared their lamps. Then the five foolish ones asked the others, 'Please give us some of your oil because our lamps are going out.' But the others replied, 'We don't have enough for all of us. Go to a shop and buy some for yourselves.'

"But while they were gone to buy oil, the bridegroom came, and those who were ready went in with him to the marriage feast, and the door was locked. Later, when the other five bridesmaids returned, they stood outside, calling, `Sir, open the door for us!' But he called back, `I don't know you!'

"So stay awake and be prepared, because you do not know the day or hour of my return" (Matthew 25:1-13).

Imagine taking a class that has only one test at the end

of the course. How would you feel if you studied very diligently for the test, but as you took it, you realized that you had studied the wrong material? In the parable of the bridesmaids, the foolish bridesmaids were unprepared for the "test." They didn't realize it at first, but when the bridegroom said, "I don't know you," they realized they had failed, and it was too late for them to enter the wedding feast. In contrast, things went very well for the wise bridesmaids. They were prepared, and they were welcomed by the bridegroom.

It is interesting to note that the foolish bridesmaids didn't understand the importance of getting to know God in relationship and were told, "I never knew you." In contrast, it is likely that the wise bridesmaids did well because they wanted to learn from God themselves and were eager to be in a relationship with Him.

The following parable of the three servants also demonstrates the importance of learning from God ourselves.

> *Jesus said, "Again, the Kingdom of Heaven can be illustrated by the story of a man going on a trip. He called together his servants and gave them money to invest for him while he was gone. He gave five bags of gold to one, two bags of gold to another, and one bag of gold to the last-dividing it in proportion to their abilities-and then left on his trip. The servant who received the five bags of gold began*

The Value and Privilege of Learning From God

immediately to invest the money and soon doubled it. The servant with two bags of gold also went right to work and doubled the money. But the servant who received the one bag of gold dug a hole in the ground and hid the master's money for safekeeping.

"After a long time their master returned from his trip and called them to give an account of how they had used his money. The servant to whom he had entrusted the five bags of gold said, 'Sir, you gave me five bags of gold to invest, and I have doubled the amount.' The master was full of praise. 'Well done, my good and faithful servant. You have been faithful in handling this small amount, so now I will give you many more responsibilities. Let's celebrate together!'

"Next came the servant who had received the two bags of gold, with the report, 'Sir, you gave me two bags of gold to invest, and I have doubled the amount.' The master said, 'Well done, my good and faithful servant. You have been faithful in handling this small amount, so now I will give you many more responsibilities. Let's celebrate together!'

"Then the servant with the one bag of gold came and said, 'Sir, I know you are a hard man, harvesting crops you didn't plant and

gathering crops you didn't cultivate. I was afraid I would lose your money, so I hid it in the earth and here it is.'

"But the master replied, 'You wicked and lazy servant! You think I'm a hard man, do you, harvesting crops I didn't plant and gathering crops I didn't cultivate? Well, you should at least have put my money into the bank so I could have some interest. Take the money from this servant and give it to the one with the ten bags of gold. To those who use well what they are given, even more will be given, and they will have an abundance. But from those who are unfaithful, even what little they have will be taken away. Now throw this useless servant into outer darkness, where there will be weeping and gnashing of teeth' (Matthew 25:14-30).

The servant who hid his money did not have a good understanding of God's character and activity in the world. Instead he thought that God was "a hard man, harvesting crops He didn't plant and gathering crops He didn't cultivate." By hiding his money, he refused to take responsibility for the things that God asked him to do. I don't know what he did after he hid the money, but it obviously wasn't what God wanted him to do, and so, overall, he completely missed out on God's best for his life. The other servants had a good understanding of God and ultimately were fruitful in

The Value and Privilege of Learning From God

the things God asked them to do. In turn they became pleasing to God. If we hope to be like these faithful servants, we truly need God as our instructor. The following verses describe God's teaching in terms of the renewing of our minds.

> *Therefore, I urge you, brothers, in view of God's mercy, to offer your bodies as living sacrifices, holy and pleasing to God-this is your spiritual act of worship.* ***Do not conform any longer to the pattern of this world, but be transformed by the renewing of your mind. Then you will be able to test and approve what God's will is-his good, pleasing and perfect will*** (Romans 12:1-2 NIV, emphasis mine).

The great thing about hanging out with God, being mentored by Him, and having Him renew our minds and mature our thinking, is that gaining His best perspective for us will positively affect the rest of our lives.

It is not surprising that God Himself recommends that we learn from Him. We can see this in the following passage.

> *Jesus said, "Come to me, all of you who are weary and carry heavy burdens, and I will give you rest. Take my yoke upon you.* ***Let me teach you****, because I am humble and gentle,*

and you will find rest for your souls. For my yoke fits perfectly, and the burden I give you is light" (Matthew 11:28-30, emphasis mine).

There are many reasons why it is of great value for each of us to learn from God—many more than I could write in this book or than I even know about. But learning from God is of great value and something I want to do in my own life. When I first entered into a relationship with God, I realized that there were many different religions and philosophies in our world. Early on, I committed to learn from God and asked Him to help me understand what is the truth. This became my ongoing request to God over the years, that He would teach me every day of my life, and that I would know truth in my inner being. If you haven't done so already, I hope you would join me and ask God to do the same for you.

The Tremendous Privilege It Is to Learn From God

People count it a privilege to meet the president of a country, a movie star, or a famous athlete. How much greater is it to meet the Creator of the universe—the One to whom we owe our very existence! I like to ponder God's greatness, although I cannot truly begin to fathom it. I have enjoyed thinking about the following verses.

The Value and Privilege of Learning From God

The LORD is exalted over all the nations, his glory above the heavens. Who is like the LORD our God, the One who sits enthroned on high, ***who stoops down to look on the heavens and the earth?*** (Psalm 113:4-6 NIV, emphasis mine)

If God is so great that it requires humility on His part to stoop down to look upon the heavens and the earth, how much farther does He have to humble Himself to be with us? And yet God loves us so much that He is willing to be intimately familiar with us in great detail. We can see this in the following verses:

O LORD, ***you have examined my heart and know everything about me.*** *You know when I sit down or stand up. You know my every thought when far away. You chart the path ahead of me and tell me where to stop and rest. Every moment you know where I am. You know what I am going to say even before I say it, LORD. You both precede and follow me. You place your hand of blessing on my head. Such knowledge is too wonderful for me, too great for me to know! I can never escape from your spirit! I can never get away from your presence! If I go up to heaven, you are there; if I go down to the place of the dead, you are there. If I ride the wings of the morning, if I dwell by the farthest oceans, even there your hand will guide me, and your strength will support me. I* *could ask the darkness to hide me and the light around me to become night-but even in darkness I cannot hide from you. To you the night shines as bright as day. Darkness and light are both alike to you. You made all the delicate, inner parts of my body and knit me together in my mother's womb. Thank you for making me so wonderfully complex! Your workmanship is marvelous-and how well I know it. You watched me as I was being formed in utter seclusion, as I was woven together in the dark of the womb. You saw me before I was born. Every day of my life was recorded in your book. Every moment was laid out before a single day had passed. How precious are your thoughts about me, O God! They are innumerable! I can't even count them; they outnumber the grains of sand! **And when I wake up in the morning, you are still with me!*** (Psalm 139:1-18, emphasis mine).

It is a great privilege to learn from the One who always loves us, is always with us, and knows everything about us—the One who knows us better than we know ourselves!

It is also a privilege to learn from the One who knows exactly what is best for us to learn. The following verses demonstrate how people loved to learn from Jesus (God), because He completely knew what He was talking about.

The Value and Privilege of Learning From God

After Jesus finished speaking, the crowds were amazed at his teaching, for he taught as one who had real authority-quite unlike the teachers of religious law (Matthew 7:18-29).

All the people hung on every word he said (Luke 19:48).

It is encouraging to know that God knows exactly what He is doing in our lives. This is certainly a contrast to being taught by someone who is only trying out their latest theories on us. God is definitely the #1 instructor of all time, with the #1 curriculum plan tailored uniquely to each of us for our very best!

Chapter 3

Practical Ways To Learn From God

Now that we have examined the importance of learning from God and why it is a tremendous privilege to do so, we now turn to the question: "How can we actually learn from God?"

PAUSE POINT

This is our first pause point in this book. I'll place these pause points throughout the book as places for you to contemplate your answers to a question or two, before I dive into some of my thoughts on a topic. If you first explore your thoughts on a topic, through a pause-point question, it may help you to think more about the issues and thus create a more meaningful reading experience for you. So, if this approach sounds good to you, please take a moment to ponder the following question before continuing to read.

Practical Ways to Learn From God

How do you go about learning from God in your own life?

If you were to ask me this question, I would likely answer by starting with the following passage from the Bible:

> *But you have received the Holy Spirit, and he lives within you, so you don't need anyone to teach you what is true. For the Spirit teaches you all things, and what he teaches is true—it is not a lie. So continue in what he has taught you, and continue to live in Christ* (1 John 2:27).

When we received forgiveness because of Jesus' work on the cross, and we in turn invited God into our hearts, God's Spirit came to live inside of us and began to teach us from within. But how does this actually take place? I'll list some of the ways with which I am familiar.

God Is a Filter

God's Spirit within us is like a filter. A filter is often used to strain out impurities from a liquid. In a similar way, our senses provide information to us by what we see, hear, and feel. As this various sensory data comes to us, God on the inside of us will act as a filter to give us the sense of which thoughts are good for us to keep, and which thoughts would be best to strain out.

Sometimes when I read or listen to something, it doesn't ring true to me. I might not be able to put my finger on what exactly wasn't right, but God within me was pointing out that something was wrong. In doing this, God helps to strain out that which isn't good for me. In some of these cases, I later learned more from God and realized what part of the statement was actually good (or at least acceptable), and what part was bad and needed to be strained out. But at the time of the initial filtering, it was good enough to just have the whole thing strained out. It is like taking a bite of apple and sensing something doesn't taste quite right. After spitting out the bad bite, it becomes apparent that there is a worm in the apple. "Learning more" is done by taking a knife and cutting up the apple. Once the part affected by the worm is removed, the rest of the apple can be quite good to eat.

God inside of us works as more than just a filter, however. He also enhances and gives insights into the data we receive. As we read or hear something, we might suddenly have an insight about it. This might be as simple as an idea dawning on us: "Oh, how about that! I didn't realize that before." Or it might be an "ah-ha" moment, in which something suddenly stands out to us and we realize it is quite significant.

God inside of us also enhances our conscience. In my own life, before I entered into a relationship with God, my sense of morality was primarily based upon the benefit I thought I would gain in doing something, versus the likelihood of and the penalty involved in getting caught. But when God came inside of me, I became much more aware of what things were good to do and what things were best to avoid.

Besides enhancing our conscience, God also enhances our common sense. He does this partly by enriching our speech and our knowledge (1 Corinthians 1:4-6). God also renews our minds and gives us a better sense of what things are practical, good to do, and pleasing to Him (Romans 12:1-2).

God works in all of us who have entered into a relationship with Him. He teaches us, causes us to grow, and helps us to think better as He filters and enhances the data we receive, our conscience, and common sense. But God can also bring very direct or extraordinary insight into our circumstances. We can see this in the following verses:

> *Then after I have poured out my rains again, I will pour out my Spirit upon all people. Your sons and daughters will prophesy. Your old men will dream dreams. Your young men will see visions. In those days, I will pour out my Spirit even on servants, men and women alike* (Joel 2:28-29).

Sometimes God communicates in ways that are even more direct than visions or dreams. For example, in

Exodus 33:11 God spoke face to face with Moses, in the same manner that a man would speak to his friend. It doesn't get much more direct than that!

These more direct forms of communication are less common than the filtering, conscience, and common sense God usually brings to our lives. For example, I have seen God teach me almost every day in these common ways. But on occasion, I have experienced more direct insight, such as the day I went to look for an apartment in a town close to where my fianceé lived. That morning, I was reading the Bible and suddenly I knew deep inside myself that the apartment I would rent would cost $250 a month. (You can probably tell from this price that this was some time ago, back in 1983!) I looked at many apartments that day, but none were renting for that exact price. When I almost ran out of time to look, I began to wonder if I had "heard" the price correctly. I kept praying for God to guide me, and as I was driving down a certain road, I suddenly felt that I shouldn't go any farther. I pulled my car over to the side of the road, but I was confused—I could not see any apartments from where I was parked. My fiancée was with me, and she had seen an "apartment-for-rent" sign on the previous block. I called and found that they indeed had an apartment for $250.

This was the first time I experienced such specific guidance from God. But there are many people who are in relationship with God who receive little or no direct guidance from Him. However, whether with extraordinary forms of guidance or none at all, I'm glad that God guides us through His filtering, our conscience, and our common sense, and that He can also give us more direct forms of guidance when He knows it is best to give it.

What Can We Do on Our Part?

It's great having the God of the universe living inside of us, guiding us, and teaching us the things that are good for us to know. But besides paying attention to His instruction, is there anything else we can do to help in this process? The following are some of the things I have found helpful to do.

1. Ask God to help our hearts be good soil for learning.
2. Take time to read the Bible. This is one of the excellent sources that God can use in teaching us.
3. Look to God for wisdom wherever we lack it.

Let's take a look at each of these three items.

Being Good Heart Soil

One thing we can do is ask God for soft hearts that can easily receive those things He is trying to teach us. This was the "good soil" in the parable of the seeds (which we looked at in Chapter 2).

> *The good soil represents the hearts of those who truly accept God's message and produce a huge harvest-thirty, sixty, or even a hundred times as much as had been planted* (Matthew 13:23).

This good soil was soft enough to receive the seed well, but the harder soil could not receive the seed.

> *For the hearts of these people are hardened, and their ears cannot hear, and they have closed their eyes-so their eyes cannot see, and their ears cannot hear, and their hearts cannot understand, and they cannot turn to me and let me heal them* (Matthew 13:15).

There is a quick and sure way to hinder our ability to learn from God: All we have to do is harden our hearts and not receive what He is teaching us. It is like a parent who is talking to a child but the child puts their fingers in their ears so that they can't hear. At one point, Jesus was instructing His disciples and saw that their hearts were becoming hardened. This is what Jesus shared with them:

> *Jesus knew what they were thinking, so he said, "Why are you so worried about having no food?* **Won't you ever learn or understand? Are your hearts too hard to take it in?**" (Mark 8:17, emphasis mine).

These verses show the relationship between having a hardened heart and not being able to learn or understand. If we harden our hearts, we can quickly stop the great things God wants to do in our lives. For this reason, God gives us the following strong warning for our benefit:

> *But never forget the warning: "Today you must listen to his voice. Don't harden your hearts against him as Israel did when they rebelled"* (Hebrews 3:15).

But if we have soft hearts, God can grant us wisdom, knowledge, and understanding, as the following verses indicate:

> *For the LORD grants wisdom! From his mouth come knowledge and understanding* (Proverbs 2:6).

> ***For wisdom will enter your heart,** and knowledge will fill you with joy* (Proverbs 2:10, emphasis mine).

The Bible As an Excellent Source

Something else we can do on our part to learn from God is to spend time reading His Word.

The Bible is a wonderful book that God has written

through people who were in a strong relationship with Him. It contains an incredible amount of great instruction for us.

We can get even more out of what we read in the Bible if we ask God to always teach us when we read, and if we then pay special attention to those things that stand out to us. As I said earlier, God inside of us works as more than just as a filter. He will also enhance and give insights into the different data we receive. As we read or hear something, we might suddenly receive an insight into it. I have found that God does this by making certain things stand out to me when I read the Bible. It is as if the text suddenly becomes set in boldface type or highlighted, even though it is really not. It is hard to describe, but if you have experienced it, then you know exactly what I am saying. If you have not experienced this yet, you may want to ask God to help you do so.

As I'm reading the Bible, when something really stands out to me, I'll pause to look at it, and I am often amazed at how it pertains to something I'm going through, or how it answers a question in my mind. This is even more amazing to me when I think of all the verses I've read over the years and how I always seem to read the one that is just right for that particular time in my life. It is mind-boggling to ponder how many details God must be using to teach me. By causing certain things to stand out to each of us, God tailors the Bible uniquely to our lives. However, there are still questions we will face in life to which we won't find direct answers in the Bible, such as what job we should take, where we should live, and exactly how we should be spending our time and money. In these situations, I find it very helpful to ask God for wisdom.

God's Wisdom As an Excellent Source

Earlier, we looked at a verse in Proverbs 2 that tells how God can bring wisdom into our hearts. If we look at a larger section of this chapter, of which this verse is a part, we will learn more about the importance of wisdom.

> *Tune your ears to wisdom, and concentrate on understanding. Cry out for insight and understanding. Search for them as you would for lost money or hidden treasure. Then you will understand what it means to fear the LORD, and you will gain knowledge of God. For the LORD grants wisdom! From his mouth come knowledge and understanding. He grants a treasure of good sense to the godly. He is their shield, protecting those who walk with integrity. He guards the paths of justice and protects those who are faithful to him.*
>
> *Then you will understand what is right, just, and fair, and you will know how to find the right course of action every time. For wisdom*

will enter your heart, and knowledge will fill you with joy. Wise planning will watch over you. Understanding will keep you safe.

Wisdom will save you from evil people, from those whose speech is corrupt (Proverbs 2:2-12).

It is good for us to tune our ears to God's wisdom! His wisdom is so important that we should seek it as if we were searching for lost money or hidden treasure.

Life is so much more difficult to navigate without God's wisdom. I have faced numerous situations as a husband, parent, friend, and employee in which I did not know what was the best thing to do. But when I eventually turned to God and asked for His wisdom, He helped me greatly in these situations. Through these experiences, I have become very fond of the following verses that tell us that anytime we are lacking in wisdom, we should ask God for His wisdom and He will graciously grant our request.

If you need wisdom—if you want to know what God wants you to do—ask him, and he will gladly tell you. He will not resent your asking. But when you ask him, be sure that you really expect him to answer, for a doubtful mind is as unsettled as a wave of the sea that is driven and tossed by the wind. People like that should not expect to receive anything from the Lord. They can't make up their minds. They waver back and forth in everything they do (James 1:5-8, emphasis mine).

I've been asking God for wisdom a lot more lately, and He is helping me to notice more quickly the gap between what I know and what would be good for me to know. Many times in the past I have felt inadequate for not knowing what to do in a situation. I have thought, *What is wrong with me? Shouldn't I know what to do here?* I have especially felt tempted to think this way when the situation didn't actually seem to be large or difficult. I'm thankful that these verses from James give me the freedom and encouragement to ask God for wisdom, no matter how small the problem might be.

Sometimes my lack of wisdom results from my not knowing the future and being faced with a decision in which such knowledge could really be useful. But I have found in these situations that just a little bit of guidance from God can go a long way. If God grants me the wisdom to know what is His best for me to do, then it definitely solves any "tiebreakers" between possible choices! It also provides an anchor for any future doubts, because even in difficult times it is easier to be at peace when I am certain that I have chosen God's best for me. When I was thinking of getting married, I desired God's guidance. I knew that there were many unforeseen variables in marriage, and I only wanted to take that step if it was God's best for me. So I asked God for wisdom and then waited for the needed confirmation from Him. When I received the "green light," so to speak, it provided a strong foundation to my married life because I was certain that getting married was what God had wanted me to do.

As I have asked God for wisdom at different times over the years, I have been amazed at His ability to provide what I have needed. Many times I have asked God for wisdom and a few months later realized that I somehow had the wisdom and understanding that I had lacked earlier. At times I could trace the exact point at which the wisdom arrived, such as through something someone said, something I read in the Bible, or even something that dawned on me as I was cutting the grass! But at other times, I had no idea how God gave me the understanding of what was best to do. Maybe I just wasn't paying attention, or perhaps He provided it just below my level of consciousness. In either case, it is amazing the incredible number of details God uses to provide what is needed.

In the following passage from James, I have wondered at times why the qualification exists that the person must expect an answer and not have a doubtful mind.

> *If you need wisdom—if you want to know what God wants you to do—ask him, and he will gladly tell you. He will not resent your asking.* **But when you ask him, be sure that you really expect him to answer, for a doubtful mind is as unsettled as a wave of**

> *the sea that is driven and tossed by the wind. People like that should not expect to receive anything from the Lord. They can't make up their minds. They waver back and forth in everything they do* (James 1:5-8, emphasis mine).

I'm not sure what the full answer is, but I do know that if we ask God for wisdom but don't trust Him to bring the answer in His way and time, we might be tempted to run ahead and not wait for God. The Bible describes many situations in which people did not ask God for His wisdom or did not wait for Him to bring the needed understanding. In these instances, the bad effects of the poor decisions that they made become obvious. There is a trust factor that is needed—trust that God will indeed bring in the needed insight in His way and time. This reminds me of the following verses that show the value of keeping in step with God.

> *If we are living now by the Holy Spirit, let us follow the Holy Spirit's leading in every part of our lives* (Galatians 5:25).

> *O Israel, how can you say the LORD does not see your troubles? How can you say God refuses to hear your case? Have you never heard or understood? Don't you know that the LORD is the everlasting God, the Creator of all the earth? He never grows faint or weary. No one can measure the depths of his understanding.*

> *He gives power to those who are tired and worn out; he offers strength to the weak. Even youths will become exhausted, and young men will give up.* ***But those who wait on the LORD will find new strength. They will fly high on wings like eagles. They will run and not grow weary. They will walk and not faint*** (Isaiah 40:27-31, emphasis mine).

God's altar can bring freedom to our lives. But it is important for us to look to God for wisdom at the altar, or we could easily sacrifice the wrong things there. With our ability to harden our hearts and rationalize our behavior, it is easy to give God a substitute for what He is asking us to do. For example, we might get very busy doing many "good" activities for Him, but miss the most important thing we could do: get to know Him. The foolish bridesmaids seemed to have this dilemma. The bridesmaids who did well were the ones who had acquired wisdom. Therefore, I think it is wise to share our full hearts' desires with God, surrender all of our desires on the altar, and attain wisdom from God as to what is best to sacrifice or to keep.

Practical Things We Can Do

In this final section, I would like to sum up and extend some of the practical aspects in this chapter. I have personally found all of these things to be very helpful for me to do. At the same time, I realize they may fit into your life somewhat differently than they do into mine. So I welcome you to join me in asking God to give us wisdom to see how these things can best fit into our lives.

1. Ask God for a soft heart and a willingness to follow His best for us.

Ultimately, the needed ability to learn from God comes from God. Asking God for this ability is a great thing for us to do.

2. Ask God to teach us through all of life and take time to read the Bible daily.

I would highly recommend that we ask God to teach us through all of life, including what we read in the Bible. When we read the Bible, God can make certain things stand out to us, and if we pause and contemplate those things, we will be amazed at how God causes those things to pertain to what we are currently going through in our daily lives.

If you have never read the Bible before, I would recommend reading the book of John first and then the entire New Testament. In order to stay consistent, I would read at least one chapter a day. God has packed the Bible with a tremendous amount of wisdom. It is like an iceberg that, at first glance, does not seem large until we understand what lies beneath the surface of the water. Each time you read through the Bible with God teaching you, you'll be amazed at how much more is below the surface. My favorite Bible translations are the New International Version and the New Living Translation. You can find these at almost any Christian bookstore. If you would like additional ideas on how to read and study the Bible, please see the appendix of this book.

3. Seek wisdom wherever we need it.

Any time we notice a gap between what we know and what would seem good for us to know, it is good for us to ask God for the needed wisdom. For those requests that take longer to be answered, we could write down what we ask for and then mark a date on our calendars a few months later for us to review those requests. When we review our lists, we may want to ask ourselves the following questions:

- Am I amazed at what I now know in regard to my requests?
- Do I know how God had me attain the needed insights?

Summary

This chapter was written to help us focus on how to learn from God. Even though we can't sit physically at Jesus' feet today as Mary did, we instead have the tremendous privilege of having His Holy Spirit dwell within us and teach us from the inside. Being able to learn from God, like Mary did, is a tremendous privilege that is key to our growing in His very best for us.

Chapter 4

Friendship With God

A high-school boy and girl fell in love for the first time. Many of their thoughts are consumed with how wonderful the other person is. When asked why they like the other person so much or what they think is so great about the other person, they may struggle to communicate clearly all of the wonderful thoughts that have permeated their minds. It's as if they have pictures in their minds of each other that are wonderful but hard to describe. As the saying goes, "A picture is worth a thousand words."

In a similar way, the heart of a deep friendship with God is a love relationship that goes beyond words. Mary had this kind of love in her heart for Jesus, which in turn gave her a strong desire to stay at His feet. If she did not have this love in her heart, I doubt she would have been so motivated to be with Him.

In this chapter, we'll explore the topic of a deep love-friendship with God. We'll do this in three main sections:
1. Some overall thoughts about friendship with God
2. How we can grow in friendship with God
3. Practical things we can do

SECTION 1

Overall Thoughts About Friendship With God

And we know that the Son of God has come, and he has given us understanding so that we can know the true God... (1 John 5:20).

You love him even though you have never seen him... (1 Peter 1:8).

To know and love God in a deep friendship is my highest goal in life. God is the best friend I could ever have, and I certainly would like for God to consider me a very close friend of His. So, this chapter on friendship with God is very near and dear to my heart. I hope that as I share my passion about this wonderful topic, you will find it of value to you in your walk with God, just as I have in mine.

Falling in Love

When I think about the high-school boy and girl that fell in love, it reminds me of my own relationship with God. Like the high-school couple, I also have wonderful thoughts in my mind about God. The high-school boy and girl will eventually begin to realize that the other has faults. But I am thankful that God is more wonderful than I know, and that the more I get to know Him, the more amazing I find Him to be! I can only scratch the surface of how wonderful He is! I am so glad that God has designed us for deep, lasting relationships with Him, and that there is no better thing He could give us than eternal friendship with Himself.

Focusing on Jesus

In my friendship with God, I find it very helpful to focus on Jesus, because He provides me with a personal contact point from which to interact with an infinite God. In Colossians 1:15, Paul wrote that Jesus is the visible image of the invisible God. So, instead of trying to relate to a huge invisible God, I am thankful that God came to the earth in the person of Jesus—Someone to whom I can very much relate. As I read in the Bible how Jesus interacted with different people, I better understand who God is. The Scriptures reveal His desires and show how He relates to people.

If someone would say to me, "Shouldn't you focus on

God the Father instead of Jesus?" I would answer, "If your life with God works well that way, great! But I personally like to focus on Jesus because He provides me with a personal point of contact with God. I also know that if I have friendship with the Son (Jesus), I have friendship with the Father, as well." The following verses show this relationship.

> *Jesus said, "Anyone who denies the Son doesn't have the Father either. But anyone who confesses the Son has the Father also"* (1 John 2:23).

> *"Where is your father?" they asked. Jesus answered, "Since you don't know who I am, you don't know who my Father is. If you knew me, then you would know my Father, too"* (John 8:19).

The following analogy is helpful in seeing how Jesus can be our personal point of contact with God. It also shows the relationship between the three parts of God (the Father, the Son [Jesus], and the Holy Spirit) but how they are all one God.

When I turn on the kitchen faucet, water keeps pouring and pouring out of it until I turn it off. How can so much water come out of such a small faucet? Because there is a whole reservoir of water behind that faucet! When we look at God, the Father is like the reservoir, the Son (Jesus) is like the faucet (the part out of which we see the water flowing), and the Holy Spirit is like the water that fills our cups. We are the cups that contain the water of God's Holy Spirit within us. God is like the water in the sense that the water is still water no matter where it is at, whether it's in the reservoir, coming out of the faucet, or in the cups. But when I walk up to the sink, the first thing I see is the faucet out of which the water is flowing, and that's my focal point for interacting with God.

Even though I find this analogy to be helpful, it quickly breaks down by not showing the perfect relationship that God has with Himself, as all three parts interact in a perfect love-friendship. God's friendship with Himself is so complete that God is not in need of our friendship, and yet in His great love for us, He invites us to join into this wonderful friendship that He has with Himself.

Now that I have explained why Jesus is the focal point of my heart in relating with an infinite God, it will make it easier for me to communicate personally about God by predominantly referring to Him as "Jesus" instead of "God" throughout the rest of this book.

Jesus As a Best Friend

PAUSE POINT
Why do you think Jesus is the best Friend that you or I could ever have?

When I look at friendship with God, I think, What qualities does Jesus have that make Him a better friend than anyone else? The following four points are a good start toward answering this question.

1) Jesus loves us perfectly.

Jesus loves me perfectly all the time. The consistency of His love is amazing! I have often looked to humans to love me consistently, and in turn, I have often been sorely disappointed. But Jesus has never faltered in His love for me. When I consider Jesus hanging on the cross paying for my sins, knowing that He could come down from the cross at any time, and yet He was willing to take all of my punishment upon Himself, I think, *Wow, what a demonstration of His amazing love for me! There is no one else who loves me like that!*

> *Jesus said, "The greatest love is shown when people lay down their lives for their friends" (John 15:13).*

> *When we were utterly helpless, Christ [Jesus] came at just the right time and died for us sinners. Now, no one is likely to die for a good person, though someone might be willing to die for a person who is especially good. But God showed his great love for us by sending Christ [Jesus] to die for us while we were still sinners (Romans 5:6-8).*

It is amazing that even when I was hostile and unloving toward God in my atheistic childhood, He had still lovingly laid down His life for me. When I had no way to attain His love, He loved me anyway and was willing to ransom me from the penalties I deserved. Jesus rescued me from those negative aspects of myself that kept me from a relationship with Him, and He continues to daily free me to walk in love and friendship with Him. I'm glad for Jesus' perfect love and for His constancy in always having that love for me. Just knowing I'm so loved has brought stability to my life. Jesus' love is the safest place for our hearts to respond to His wonderful invitation to a deep friendship. In fact, it is the safest place for relationship, since Jesus will never hurt us in relationship as most humans will.

2) Jesus is always there for us and is willing to help us.

Jesus has the wonderful friendship quality of availability. If we are going through a hard time, will our friends always be there for us? If we are fortunate to have good friends, they might be there for us most of the time. But Jesus is there for us all of the time. Not only is His presence with us, but He also indwells us by His Holy Spirit. Talk about intimacy and closeness! When we first entered into relationship with Him, at the very point when we received Him, He literally took up residency within us. I'm glad that God is with us all the time!

Friends will lend a listening ear, but Jesus is with us 24-7 to listen to us share with Him those things that are troubling us or are on our minds. Not only is He there to listen, but He can also give us strength, insight, peace, and healing. I'm glad that when He listens to us, He not only cares and understands, but He does so perfectly and completely. The following verses speak about the care He has for us:

> *Give all your worries and cares to God, for he cares about what happens to you* (1 Peter 5:7).

> *Don't worry about anything; instead, pray about everything. Tell God what you need, and thank him for all he has done. If you do this, you will experience God's peace, which is far more wonderful than the human mind can understand. His peace will guard your hearts and minds as you live in Christ Jesus* (Philippians 4:6-7).

3) Jesus is never a "jerk."

All of us have the capability of being a "jerk!" There are times when we become stressed and tired and are irritable toward others and treat them in ways we wouldn't want to be treated. Unlike us, Jesus will never be a jerk. He doesn't become tired and irritable. He won't go from being in a good mood and accepting us to quickly changing to a bad mood and then rejecting us. Instead, He has unconditional love toward us all the time. I'm glad that Jesus is always a solid and consistent Friend. Jesus is definitely the rock of my relationship with Him!

I like the following Scripture passage because it speaks of Jesus' consistency.

> *Have you never heard or understood? Don't you know that the LORD is the everlasting God, the Creator of all the earth?* **He never grows faint or weary.** *No one can measure the depths of his understanding. He gives power to those who are tired and worn out; he offers strength to the weak. Even youths will become exhausted, and young men will give up. But those who wait on the LORD will find new strength. They will fly high on wings like eagles. They will run and not grow weary. They will walk and not faint* (Isaiah 40:28-31, emphasis mine).

4) Jesus is the most personal Friend.

Jesus is the most personal Friend we could ever have. If we open our hearts wide to Him, He won't act like some humans do and suddenly begin to take us for granted, try to use us, or treat us badly. Instead, as we open our hearts wider to Him, we'll find that He has already been at that deeper level and will fully meet us in a heart-to-heart friendship there. It is fascinating that we are the ones who are limited in how far we can go in relationship with Him, but Jesus is not limited in His relationship with us. We have a totally safe place to fully open wide our hearts, a place to share all of our desires and concerns, a place where it is safe to live with the best possible Friend, Jesus.

Even though Jesus is my best Friend, I treat my relationship with Him with tremendous respect. I realize that although Jesus is the best Friend I will ever have, He is also the God of the universe—a God who is awesome, powerful, and holy. Therefore, interacting with Jesus is a little bit like interacting with electricity. If I am dealing with high voltage, I definitely want to be insulated! In the Old Testament, David learned this lesson the hard way when his friend Uzzah touched the ark of God and was struck dead instantly. This event frightened David, but it also caused him to have an even greater respect for God.

> *But when they arrived at the threshing floor of Nacon, the oxen stumbled, and Uzzah put out his hand to steady the Ark of God. Then the LORD's anger blazed out against Uzzah for doing this, and God struck him dead beside the Ark of God.*
>
> *David was now afraid of the LORD and asked, "How can I ever bring the Ark of the LORD*

back into my care?" So David decided not to move the Ark of the LORD into the City of David. He took it instead to the home of Obed-edom of Gath. The Ark of the LORD remained there with the family of Obed-edom for three months, and the LORD blessed him and his entire household.

Then King David was told, "The LORD has blessed Obed-edom's home and everything he has because of the Ark of God." So David went there and brought the Ark to the City of David with a great celebration. After the men who were carrying it had gone six steps, they stopped and waited so David could sacrifice an ox and a fattened calf. And David danced before the LORD with all his might, wearing a priestly tunic. So David and all Israel brought up the Ark of the LORD with much shouting and blowing of trumpets (2 Samuel 6:6-7, 9-15).

The first time I read this passage, I was shocked by it. Had God maintained His perfect quality of love at the point when He struck Uzzah dead? Now I realize that I was looking at the wrong side of the coin. On the one side of the coin, God was perfectly maintaining His love, as He always does. But on the other side of the coin, His tremendous holiness is so great that no one can approach Him without being properly insulated by His forgiveness through the blood He shed on the cross.

At times, God's perfect holiness is hard for me to grasp. Jesus' perfection and greatness are too much for my small human brain to comprehend. When John the Baptist encountered Jesus, he sensed Jesus' greatness and concluded that he himself was not even worthy to be Jesus' servant or carry His sandals. This Jesus is the One to whom we owe our very existence-as well as the existence of the entire universe! He is so great that we don't even deserve to carry His sandals for Him. And yet, if we approach Him in humility (and in light of His payment on the cross), Jesus says that He desires to gather us to Himself as a mother hen gathers her chicks under her wings. (See Matthew 23:37.)

This is the kind of intimacy that God would like to have with us—He wants us to be close to His heart. But again, the context must be that we approach God from a place of being "insulated." For example, I love drawing close to Jesus, but I always do so with an attitude of reverence and in acknowledgement of His tremendous power. Christ can do as He pleases, and I do not take lightly His mercy toward me. But I also know that I can be close to Him because of His blood that was shed for me on the cross. So, I look to Jesus to help me keep from being judgmental, angry, or manipulative toward Him. Instead I hope to care for Jesus as He does for me: I desire to be an excellent friend to Him.

More Than a Celebrity

People often get excited when they see someone famous. If they actually get to meet the person, their excitement level may skyrocket. But consider how much greater is the privilege of having your best Friend be the God of the universe! The One who is all powerful, totally loving, and the most wonderful Friend that I could ever have is the Creator of all things!

People often do not fully realize how important or valuable another person is to them until that person dies. At the funeral, they often regret not having told the person how much they valued and appreciated them. In a similar way, because Jesus is always with us, it is easy to under-appreciate Him. I wonder, How would I feel if this were the last day that Jesus would ever be alive? What would I want to say to Him? How would I feel at the thought of having to live life without Him being with me all the time?

PAUSE POINT
If Jesus were only to be around for the rest of today, what would you want to tell Him?

Side note: *In being limited to one-way communication in this book, I miss out on hearing your thoughts on what I've been writing. I would especially love to hear your response to this Pause Point. (It would be great if we could both take a few minutes to write down our answers. I would enjoy hearing yours, and then I could share with you...)*

Here is what I would say to Him: *I am so thankful for*

You, Jesus. Thank You for being my best Friend and for always being with me. Thank You for teaching me and helping me to grow in Your love and friendship qualities. I sure am going to miss You tremendously!

I am very thankful that Jesus will never die and that He will never cease being my best Friend! Every year I find my appreciation of Him growing more and more in my heart, both for who He is and for the things He does. I'm thankful that the more I get to know Him, the more wonderful I find Him to be!

Knowing and Loving Jesus

I've asked Jesus a number of times to help me in the writing of this chapter. It is truly the "diamond" of this book in that it points to the greatest focus that we could ever have in life: to know and love Jesus. If this is the focus of your life, then I am excited for you, because with such a wonderful focus, not only do you have the best (Jesus), but I know He will also bring good things to the entirety of your life.

I'd like to end this section with a few Bible passages that point to the value of knowing and loving Jesus. Instead of putting my comments before each passage, as I typically do, I'll first give you the chance to read the passage and see what stands out to you. I'll then share those things that stand out to me, especially from the emphasized portions. The first of these passages is the main scripture upon which this book is based.

> *As Jesus and the disciples continued on their way to Jerusalem, they came to a village where a woman named Martha welcomed them into her home. Her sister,* **Mary, sat at the Lord's feet, listening to what he taught.** *But Martha was worrying over the big dinner she was preparing. She came to Jesus and said, "Lord, doesn't it seem unfair to you that my sister just sits here while I do all the work? Tell her to come and help me."*
>
> *But the Lord said to her, "My dear Martha, you are so upset over all these details!* **There is really only one thing worth being concerned about. Mary has discovered it—and I won't take it away from her**" (Luke 10:38-42, emphasis mine).

I really like how Jesus affirmed Mary's focus on being with Him and listening to what He had to say. As I said earlier, these verses provide us with keys to get to know, learn from, and love Jesus even more.

> *When Jesus had finished saying all these things, he looked up to heaven and said, "Father, the time has come. Glorify your Son so he can give glory back to you. For you have given him authority over everyone in all the*

> earth. He gives eternal life to each one you have given him. **And this is the way to have eternal life-to know you, the only true God, and Jesus Christ, the one you sent to earth.** I brought glory to you here on earth by doing everything you told me to do. And now, Father, bring me into the glory we shared before the world began (John 17:1-5, emphasis mine).

> And we know that the Son of God has come, and he has given us understanding **so that we can know the true God.** And now we are in God because we are in his Son, Jesus Christ. He is the only true God, and he is eternal life (1 John 5:20, emphasis mine).

The very definition of eternal life focuses on getting to know God. In other parts of the Bible, this definition is expanded to include spending eternity with Jesus in heaven. But if friendship with Jesus is missed, then this main point is missed.

> One of the teachers of religious law was standing there listening to the discussion. He realized that Jesus had answered well, so he asked, "Of all the commandments, which is the most important?"

> Jesus replied, **"The most important commandment is this: `Hear, O Israel! The Lord our God is the one and only Lord. And you**

must love the Lord your God with all your heart, all your soul, all your mind, and all your strength.' The second is equally important: 'Love your neighbor as yourself.' No other commandment is greater than these" (Mark 12:28-31, emphasis mine).

The greatest commandment given to us—to love God—is not a burdensome law that is imposed on me. Instead, I see it as a tremendous privilege and freedom. It directs me to one of the most important elements needed for a good friendship with Jesus: having love in my heart for Him.

SECTION 2
How We Can Grow in Friendship with God

Now that we have explored the overall topic of friendship with Jesus, let's take a look at several practical points on how we can actually grow in our friendship with Him.

1) Having an Open Heart Toward Jesus

In order to have a deep friendship with Jesus, one thing we need is an open heart. In Chapter 2, we looked at the parable of the seeds. The good soil was soft enough to receive the seed well. If we are going to have a heart-to-heart friendship with Jesus, then the soil of our heart needs to be soft and receptive to Him.

This concept also applies to human relationships. A certain amount of openness of heart is required for good relationships. In Paul's relationship with the Corinthians, he realized this key element was lacking.

> *Oh, dear Corinthian friends! We have spoken honestly with you.* ***Our hearts are open to you.*** *If there is a problem between us, it is not because of a lack of love on our part, but because you have withheld your love from us. I am talking now as I would to my own children.* ***Open your hearts to us!*** (2 Corinthians 6:11-13, emphasis mine).

There are many concepts we understand from our human relationships, including the value of openness, that we can apply to our relationship with Jesus. I hope you find the following exercise helpful to see some of these correlations.

Exercise Scenario 1
Think of someone who has been hostile or critical toward you.

How do you feel about how this person has treated you?

Exercise Scenario 2

Now think of a person who has been outwardly friendly to you and even greets you with a smile, but internally they seem to stiff-arm you and keep you at a distance. They may be polite to you, but they do not really share themselves with you, nor are they interested in your sharing yourself with them. On the surface, this person seems to be "with" you, but in reality, they are far away.

How do you feel about how this person has treated you?

Exercise Scenario 3
Now think of a person who has not only been friendly to you, but who has also made time for you and listened to you. This person is willing to share their heart with you at a deep level. They also appreciate when you share your heart with them, and they listen carefully. This person does not try to one-up you but is kind to you. You count this person as your friend.

How do you feel about how this person has treated you?

Let's apply each of these scenarios to our friendship with Jesus.

Scenario 1:
If we treated Jesus the way the first person treated us, we would tend to be critical of God and hold things against Him. If we were really honest with ourselves,

we would realize that we have actually had some very mean thoughts toward Him. Deep down, we really wouldn't think that God has our best interests in mind, and we would conclude that we would be better off keeping our distance from Him. Obviously, we wouldn't have much of a relationship with God.

Scenario 2:
If we treated Jesus the way the second person treated us, it might look like this: We would say our prayers and do "good" deeds, but we would never truly draw near to God in relationship. Instead, we would put up internal walls to keep God at arms' length. We would have bought into the deception that it is best to keep God from intruding upon our lives. We would think we'd be better off if we could "do our own thing" without God's guidance or interference. If we were really honest with ourselves, we would realize that our relationship with God consists of duty, but we are not that interested in friendship with Him.

Scenario 3:
If we treated Jesus the way the third person treated us, it might look like this: We would know Jesus as our best Friend. We would know that He only has good desires and intentions for us and that He loves us all the time. We would know that Jesus would never hurt us, and so we'd feel safe to draw near to Him and share the intimacy of our heart with Him. We would enjoy sitting at His feet in His presence. We would count on Him as our best Friend.

I hope your participation in this exercise has been helpful. I also hope that if we were to ask Jesus, "How do You feel about how we have treated You?" that He would reply that we have been His true friends.

One of the keys for us to grow in this type of relationship is to have an open heart toward Jesus. Asking Jesus to open our hearts to Him is one of the "how-to" keys to this treasure.

2) Inviting Jesus Into the Entirety of Our Lives and Everywhere We Go

Throughout this book, we have seen the importance of asking God to teach us in all of life. Similarly, it is also good to invite Jesus to go with us wherever we go. You might ask, "Isn't Jesus with us all of the time?" Technically He is, because He is always with us, but just because Jesus is with us does not mean we are with Him in relationship. It is like driving or walking somewhere with another person. Just because we are in close proximity to each other and even on the same route, we might not talk or even have a deep friendship with each other. It is completely different to truly go somewhere with another person when we are in a relationship with them. When a police officer takes a prisoner to jail, they go there together, but there is a good chance that the prisoner has a hostile attitude toward the police officer. In contrast, two people can take a trip together and deeply enjoy each other as they travel. I love to invite Jesus to go with me wherever I go. In the morning, I wake up and say, "Good morning, Jesus! I warmly invite You into my entire day and ask that You would help me to stay with You in my heart." At different times throughout the day, I invite Jesus to join me, such as when I go to work or to the store.

Moses felt the same way about being with Jesus. In Exodus 33, Moses told God that he only wanted to go to the Promised Land if God would go with him and the Israelites. If God didn't go with them, then Moses didn't want to take even a step in that direction. God was pleased with Moses and granted his request, because He knew him on a personal friendship level.

In this passage, we also find that Joshua liked to hang out in the Tent of Meeting, where God's presence was. It is no surprise that later in the Bible, Joshua is described as pleasing to God and doing well in God's best for him.

This desire to hang out with Jesus is captured nicely by a song written by Silverwind.

By His Spirit

I've heard stories of heaven, pavement made of gold.
Ageless beauty forever, that never grows old.
But if I got there only to find that, Jesus,
    You were not up there…

Goodbye wings, angel things.
Heaven is being with you.
There's nothing I'd rather do.
There is nothing better, knowing You is heaven.
There is nothing better, loving You forever, Jesus.

Heaven holds only wishes, making dreams come true.
Heaven has to be Jesus, just being with You.
There is no laughter or joy in the music.
Jesus, if You are not there, then the song is all wrong.

Heaven is being with You.
There's nothing I'd rather do.
There is nothing better, knowing You is heaven.
There is nothing better, loving You forever, Jesus.[1]

Inviting Jesus into all of life and hanging out with Him in our hearts is key to growing in our friendship with Him.[1]

3) Spending Quality Time with Jesus

One thing I find very helpful in my friendship with Jesus is to set aside time each day to spend alone with Him. Human friendships grow more deeply when people take quality time to talk with and enjoy each other, such as at mealtimes. Friendship can still take place when everyone is busy with cutting the grass, doing the laundry, and preparing meals. But being busy all the time without spending quality time together tends to take its toll on relationships. It's the same in our relationship with Jesus. It is good to invite Him to go with us wherever we go and ask Him to help us remain with Him in our hearts, but it is also important to spend quality time alone with Him in order for our friendship with Him to deepen.

In order to stay consistent, I find it helpful to set aside a certain time each day for me to be alone with Jesus. I try to be practical about this by picking a time when I can find a quiet place and am not likely to fall asleep. For me, this time works best right after my children go to bed. It is quieter and yet it is not immediately before I go to sleep. If I wait until right before I go to sleep, my time with Jesus may be too relaxing for me to stay awake!

During this time with Jesus, I usually read a few chapters of the Bible and pay special attention to those things that seem to stand out to me. When something does stand out, I pause and consider what it means. This is how Jesus often communicates with me—by causing His Word to stand out to me and helping me to understand how it pertains to my life. At some of these "pause points," I then communicate with Jesus by sharing what is on my heart with regard to the topic at hand. This includes sharing with Him my concerns or desires, or thanking Him for what the scripture passage has revealed about Him.

One of the great riches of the Bible is that it reveals

who God is, what He desires, and how He relates to people. Just as I like to focus on Jesus as my personal contact point with an infinite God, I also like to focus on how He interacts with others. Although I've read the entire Bible from cover to cover many times, I especially like to read the Gospels (Matthew, Mark, Luke, and John), paying special attention to how Jesus cares for and interacts with so many people. I really enjoy the accounts of His close friendships with people such as John, Mary, Martha, and Lazarus.

> *After he had said this, Jesus was troubled in spirit and testified, "I tell you the truth, one of you is going to betray me." His disciples stared at one another, at a loss to know which of them he meant. One of them,* **the disciple [John] whom Jesus loved, was reclining next to him.** *Simon Peter motioned to this disciple and said, "Ask him which one he means."* **Leaning back against Jesus,** *he asked him, "Lord, who is it?"* (John 13:21-25 NIV, emphasis mine).

> *After he had said this, he went on to tell them,* **"Our friend Lazarus** *has fallen asleep; but I am going there to wake him up." His disciples replied, "Lord, if he sleeps, he will get better." Jesus had been speaking of his death, but his disciples thought he meant natural sleep* (John 11:11-13, emphasis mine).

Note: *The entire chapter of John 11 gives a wonderful account of Jesus' close friendship with Mary, Martha, and Lazarus. I won't repeat it here, but feel free to read it on your own if you are interested.*

My quality time with Jesus is the part of my day I look forward to the most. I don't see this time as just reading a book (the Bible), but more as having a spiritual meal with God in which He makes the words come alive to my heart.

> *Jesus said, "The Scriptures say, 'People need more than bread for their life; they must **feed on every word of God**'"* (Matthew 4:4, emphasis mine).

Without food, the body becomes weak. Without spiritual food, the spirit becomes weak, and we lose our spiritual vitality and closeness with God. As Jesus makes His Word alive to my heart, it becomes a great strength to my life. I also just enjoy being with Him. That is why it is my favorite time of the day!

Having alone time with Jesus may work a little differently in your life than it does in mine. A different time might suit you better, such as your lunch break. You might find that crowded places work well for you, such as on a bus or train commute to and from work. You might go about reading the Bible differently or share your heart with Jesus differently than I do. But if you haven't done this before, I highly recommend it. It is more valuable than I could possibly describe. If you haven't done so already, you may want to ask Jesus to show you how to have consistent quality time with Him in your life. It is such a key to having a quality friendship with God.

4) Being with Jesus and Sharing Our Hearts With Him

My quality alone time with Jesus is a critical part of my friendship with Jesus, but aside from this time with Him, I like to "hang out" with Jesus at other times, as well. I enjoy silently basking in His presence. I sometimes do this when I find myself awake in the middle of the night, while I am driving to and from work, or on those rare days that I can start my day leisurely and spend extra time in bed just being in His presence. It is great to be able to spend time with a friend who loves me so completely.

After a time of silence, I often wind up naturally sharing with Jesus those things that seem to be on my mind or heart, just as I might do with a good human friend. This includes my deepest heart's desires and concerns.

David was a good friend of God's. God said that David was a man after His own heart—a nice compliment for David! David wrote in Psalm 62:

O my people, trust in him at all times. Pour out your heart to him, for God is our refuge (Psalm 62:8).

Why would David encourage other people to pour out their hearts to God? If Jesus already knows everything in our hearts, then why is it good for us to share our hearts with Him? Jesus certainly doesn't need to hear us say anything, does He? Because we know that Jesus only wants our very best (because He completely loves us), then what good things would He want to bring from our sharing our hearts with Him?

PAUSE POINT

Do you have any ideas why Jesus would want us to pour our hearts out to Him?

Part of the answer to this question can be found in human relationships. If I have something on my mind that has been troubling me, and if you are compassionate and have a good listening ear, when I share with you, it can help to free me up. For starters, just by sharing with you, I may realize more fully what has been troubling me. And sometimes just acknowledging the fact that something is troubling can be a step toward dealing with it. This sharing can also help to build a deeper friendship between us. In a similar way, it is freeing to share with Jesus what is on my heart and mind. It is wonderful to share with the One who completely knows and loves me, and it helps to grow my friendship with Him.

I like the following verses that encourage us to share our hearts with Jesus. You may recognize these verses from earlier in this book.

> *Then Jesus said, "Come to me, all of you who are weary and carry heavy burdens, and I will give you rest. Take my yoke upon you. Let me teach you, because I am humble and gentle, and you will find rest for your souls. For my yoke fits perfectly, and the burden I give you is light"* (Matthew 11:28-30).

> **Give all your worries and cares to God,** *for he cares about what happens to you* (1 Peter 5:7, emphasis mine).

> *Don't worry about anything; instead,* **pray about everything. Tell God what you need, and thank him for all he has done.** *If you do this, you will* **experience God's peace,** *which is far more wonderful than the human mind can understand. His peace will guard your hearts and minds as you live in Christ Jesus* (Philippians 4:6-7).

It is wonderful that Jesus is willing to shoulder the burdens of our heart! He is willing for us to roll them onto Him. As I've done this at various times, I've noticed that after giving the burden to Him, different prayers will come into my heart, and I'll ask Jesus for His help or wisdom about those things that I have shared. This is an encouraging process, as He gives me peace in exchange for my burdens, and He gives me prayers that prove helpful over time.

Besides sharing my burdens, I also like to share my heart's desires with Jesus. For example, I might say, *Dear Jesus, I would really love to see a certain thing happen for myself or for someone else.* Or I might pray, *I ask for Your help with this certain thing.* Instead of trying to demand that Jesus take action, I simply give my desire to Him and ask Him to do what He would. In other words, I follow 1 Corinthians 13:5: Love does not demand its own way.

A friend of mine named Pam had an interesting experience a few months after she entered into a relationship with Jesus. Pam had shared with Jesus her desire that her son would help out more around the house. She didn't ask Jesus to do anything about it; she simply shared with Him the desire of her heart. A week or two later, her son asked if he could help clean the house, even though Pam had never talked with him about the situation. Pam's son was so diligent that he even lay on his back to vacuum the grill of the refrigerator! Later Pam remembered how she had shared her heart's desire with God, and she was amazed at what had occurred with her son.

Over the years I have shared many desires with Jesus and have seen Him bring about wonderful things, just like Pam. Other times I have shared with Him, but never saw Him make a change in that particular area. But whether Jesus brings about wonderful things or seemingly nothing, I trust that He knows the very best for my life. I also know that it is healthy for me to pour out my heart to Him, regardless of the outcome.

As I share my heart with Jesus, I try to be very honest with Him about my thoughts and feelings. If I hold back on being honest, I know it will only hinder me, but at the same time, I am careful with my honesty. I realize that like all of us, I can be tempted to judge Jesus or hold things against Him, just like I can be tempted to judge people and hold things against them. But to do so is a relational violation and does not treat Jesus as a Friend. I've heard some people claim that being angry with God is acceptable, and even that it is good to express your anger toward Him. Personally I do not think this is wise. Instead, it is better to identify such thoughts and feelings as being wrong, and to ask Jesus for forgiveness of such attitudes. Because the greatest thing I can do is to love God, when I share my heart with Him, I want to do so respectfully and with love toward Him. I want to treat Jesus with the same kind of love that He shows to me. But within this context, I find it very helpful to be honest with Him.

My desire is that Jesus would help us to enjoy His presence and that we would pour out our hearts to Him. This is an important key to our growing in friendship with Jesus. So, whether you know Jesus' presence in a great way or hardly at all, and whether or not sharing your heart with Him comes easy to you, I welcome you to join me in asking Jesus for the following things and then see what He is willing to do on your behalf.

- Please help me to know You in a greater way and to just enjoy being with You.
- Please help me to completely share my heart with You.
- Please help me to be a good friend to You.

5) Having Our Hearts Cleansed

There are many things that can hinder our friendship with Jesus. In the parable of the seeds, we saw that there were thorns that grew up and hindered some of the plants from growing well. In the same way, there are many ways in which we can cause the soil of our hearts to not respond well to God in relationship.

Consider the following analogy: Our thoughts are like a stream that flows from our mind to our spiritual heart, which is like a pond. If we have bad thoughts, they will flow down the stream and contaminate the pond. If we harden our heart, even more pollution forms in the pond. Our spiritual eyes are at the bottom of our heart, and they look up through the pond toward Jesus. If the pond of our heart becomes polluted, it clouds the water and makes it difficult for us to see Him or sense His presence with us. Jesus described the important correlation between a "clean pond" and seeing Him, when He said, "God blesses those whose hearts are pure, for they will see God" (Matthew 5:8).

So, what do we do if our hearts are polluted? Fortunately, if we come before Jesus, ask Him to search us and show us if we have done anything wrong, confess those things to Him, and ask Him to forgive us based on His payment for us on the cross, then Jesus will not only clean out the pond of our heart, but He will also cleanse the stream of our mind, as well.

> *This is the message he has given us to announce to you: God is light and there is no darkness in him at all. So we are lying if we say we have fellowship with God but go on living in spiritual darkness. We are not living in the truth. But if we are living in the light of God's presence, just as Christ is, then we have fellowship with each other, and the blood of Jesus, his Son, cleanses us from every sin. If we say we have no sin, we are only fooling ourselves and refusing to accept the truth.* **But if we confess our sins to him, he is faithful and just to forgive us and to cleanse us from every wrong.** *If we claim we have not sinned, we are calling God a liar and showing that his word has no place in our hearts* (1John 1:5-10, emphasis mine).

In verse 9, the word "sin" is the Bible term for what I called "pollution" in the analogy. If we aren't willing to turn to God, and instead we hold onto sinful thoughts or desires, then they will isolate us from truly experiencing Jesus and His love for us. The Bible frequently emphasizes the importance of dealing with sin. If we don't deal with the sin in our lives, it will greatly hinder us from getting to know Jesus or be pleasing to Him.

So, what type of sin can pollute the pond? First John 2 provides a number of helpful examples.

> *My dear children, I am writing this to you so that you will not sin. But if you do sin, there is someone to plead for you before the Father. He is Jesus Christ, the one who pleases God completely. He is the sacrifice for our sins. He takes away not only our sins but the sins of all the world.*
>
> *And how can we be sure that we belong to him? By obeying his commandments. If someone says, "I belong to God," but doesn't obey God's commandments, that person is a liar and does not live in the truth. But those who obey God's word really do love him. That is the way to know whether or not we live in him. Those who say they live in God should live their lives as Christ [Jesus] did.*

Dear friends, I am not writing a new commandment, for it is an old one you have always had, right from the beginning. **This commandment—to love one another—is** *the same message you heard before. Yet it is also new. This commandment is true in Christ and is true among you, because the darkness is disappearing and the true light is already shining.*

If anyone says, "I am living in the light," but hates a Christian brother or sister, that person is still living in darkness. Anyone who loves other Christians is living in the light and does not cause anyone to stumble. **Anyone who hates a Christian brother or sister is living and walking in darkness.** *Such a person is lost, having been blinded by the darkness* (1 John 2:1-11, emphasis mine).

Because the greatest commandments are to love God and to love our neighbors as ourselves, it is not surprising that any violation of love constitutes sin. If I judge someone, hold something against them, or even hate them, this is a relational violation of love, and it will, in turn, harm my relationship with Jesus. For my own sake, Jesus wants me to be free of such sins so that I can operate as I was designed to operate-to live life with His love flowing through me.

Do not love the world or anything in the world. If anyone loves the world, the love of *the Father is not in him. For everything in the world—**the cravings of sinful man, the lust of his eyes and the boasting of what he has and does**—comes not from the Father but from the world. The world and its desires pass away, but the man who does the will of God lives forever* (1 John 2:15-17 NIV, emphasis mine).

If we become arrogant or lust after different things in our hearts, we pollute the pond. It is important for us to look to Jesus to help us think and desire only good things, but even in doing so, inevitably we will still sin. Therefore, it is good for the ponds of our hearts to be cleansed on a regular basis. I like to do this daily. Each morning, I ask Jesus if there is anything I've done wrong, and then I wait to see if He causes anything to stand out to me. If so, I confess these things, and ask Him to forgive me according to His payment for my sins on the cross. I then thank Jesus for His forgiveness. This process is another key to growing in friendship with Him.

6) Being Wholehearted

How would it have been if the high-school boy and girl that we looked at earlier in this chapter only had a slight desire to be together? Would their relationship look the same? Would they still have such wonderful thoughts about each other? Would they still look for any opportunity to be together?

In a similar way, to have a good friendship with Jesus we need to be wholehearted toward Him. If we lack this wholeheartedness, then other things in life will tend to crowd out our hearts and distract us from our "first love" for God. The importance of being wholehearted is seen in what Jesus stated as the greatest commandment:

> *You must love the Lord your God **with all your heart**, all your soul, and all your mind* (Matthew 22:37-38, emphasis mine).

If we hold back our hearts from Jesus, it is like pushing the brake in a car until it comes to a stop. A car is much easier to steer if it is moving; it is nearly impossible to steer if it is stopped. Instead of pushing the brake, if we have a warm heart toward Jesus and are wholehearted in following His best for us, then He can much more easily steer us in good directions for our lives.

Because Jesus only wants the best for us, if we are not wholehearted toward Him, it will only hinder the great things He wants to bring forth in our lives. Therefore, being wholehearted is one of the keys to pleasing Him. The following verses show how Jesus feels about those who are not wholehearted toward Him.

> *Jesus said, "I know all the things you do, that you are neither hot nor cold. I wish you were one or the other! But since you are like*

lukewarm water, I will spit you out of my mouth! *You say, 'I am rich. I have everything I want. I don't need a thing!' And you don't realize that you are wretched and miserable and poor and blind and naked. I advise you to buy gold from me-gold that has been purified by fire. Then you will be rich. And also buy white garments so you will not be shamed by your nakedness. And buy ointment for your eyes so you will be able to see. I am the one who corrects and disciplines everyone I love.* **Be diligent and turn from your indifference.**

"*Look! Here I stand at the door and knock. If you hear me calling and open the door, I will come in, and we will share a meal as friends. I will invite everyone who is victorious to sit with me on my throne, just as I was victorious and sat with my Father on his throne. Anyone who is willing to hear should listen to the Spirit and understand what the Spirit is saying to the churches*" (Revelation 3:15-22, emphasis mine).

Being wholehearted in following Jesus can keep us from making a common mistake: to substitute people for what only Jesus should predominantly be in our lives. If we do this, we will ultimately be disappointed with others because they cannot meet the deepest needs of our lives like Jesus can. For example, Jesus is the Source of love, and if our hearts are with Him first, then we will get "tanked up" with His perfectly constant love, and we will be able to have His love flow through our hearts to others. But if we first give our hearts to other people and look to them for perfect love, then we will surely be disappointed! We may even be tempted to manipulate other people to try to get them to love us more. So, when Jesus says that we should love God with our whole hearts, He is telling us how to have true freedom. Only if we truly love God first can we be in the place to have more of His love in our hearts for others.

So then, one of the keys to our growing in friendship with Jesus is to be wholehearted toward Him: to draw near to Him in our heart, have Him first in our heart, and have love in our heart for Him. If you have not already asked Jesus to help you with these things, then I welcome you to do so without hesitation.

Asking Jesus for these things solves a dilemma that I have had, and that a number of others have had, as well. There are times when I have felt a lack of desire to have Jesus first in my life. At these times, I've wondered what I should do, because without this in my heart, it seemed much harder to follow Him in all of His best for me. But then I read the following verses:

> *So I advise you to live according to your new life in the Holy Spirit. Then you won't be doing what your sinful nature craves. The old sinful nature loves to do evil, which is just opposite*

from what the Holy Spirit wants. **And the Spirit gives us desires** *that are opposite from what the sinful nature desires. These two forces are constantly fighting each other, and your choices are never free from this conflict. But when you are directed by the Holy Spirit, you are no longer subject to the law* (Galatians 5:16-18, emphasis mine).

From these verses, I learned that Jesus can give us good desires through His Holy Spirit within us. So, when we feel that we are lacking good desires in our heart, we can ask Jesus to remove the bad desires from our heart and give us good desires instead.

7) Looking to Jesus to Build the Relationship

There is much more to friendship with Jesus than I've described in this chapter or even than I know! Looking to Jesus to build our relationship with Him, is probably the most important point of all, for in reality, I myself can't grow my relationship with God—only God can enable me to grow in relationship with Him. And Jesus alone knows how to best accomplish this.

Therefore, it is good for us to look to Jesus and ask Him to grow a close friendship between us and Himself, and then for us to seek Him for this treasure.

Friendship With God

Jesus said, "Keep on asking, and you will be given what you ask for. Keep on looking, and you will find. Keep on knocking, and the door will be opened. For everyone who asks, receives. Everyone who seeks, finds. And the door is opened to everyone who knocks. You parents-if your children ask for a loaf of bread, do you give them a stone instead? Or if they ask for a fish, do you give them a snake? Of course not! If you sinful people know how to give good gifts to your children, how much more will your heavenly Father give good gifts to those who ask him" (Matthew 7:7-11).

It is so important for us to seek Jesus, to ask Him to build our friendship with Him, and to help us to live life as He knows is best for us to do. Writing this book has reminded me what a tremendous privilege it is to have a close friendship with Jesus, the God of the universe! The years I spent as an atheist, out on my own, not knowing why I existed, and being away from God, is so different from what I experience now. I am so thankful that the Ruler of this universe is Jesus and not a distant or malevolent entity, and that Jesus truly has my very best interests at heart-friendship with Him.

If you don't know how to seek Jesus for this, you could start by praying this prayer:

Please grow in my life a wonderful friendship with

You. Please help me to be a very good friend to You. Please help me to know You in a great way. Thanks.

To know Jesus is with us and to have a close friendship with Him are gifts that each of us may receive in different measures. In other words, friendship with Him might come easier to some of us than others. But regardless of the measure we receive, it is always good to ask for a large measure! Because friendship with Jesus is the greatest gift in life, I have asked Him to give me as much of this gift as He is willing to give me, and to enable me to grow in an excellent friendship with Him. If you haven't done so already, I invite you to ask Jesus to give you these same wonderful things.

SECTION 3
Practical Things We Can Do

This section summarizes and discusses further the practical aspects of growing in our friendship with God. Although most of these items have already been mentioned in this chapter, this section provides a summarized reference.

These ideas are not intended to be a "law," telling us what we must do to have friendship with Jesus. Instead, I hope that we would greatly value doing these things, and that they would be of great benefit to us. So, if you have not done so already, you may want to join me in asking Jesus to teach us how these can best fit into our lives.

Friendship With God

I have found the following things to be very helpful in my growing friendship with Jesus. I welcome you to join me in doing these as well.

1. Ask Jesus for:
   a. An open heart that is good heart soil.
   b. An infilling of a tremendous measure of Himself (His Holy Spirit). The more we have of Him inside us, the more we will get to know Him and live lives that are pleasing to Him.
   c. A greater realization of His presence.
   d. A strong friendship with Him.

2. When Jesus makes something alive to you, look to Him to keep you from hardening your heart (i.e., becoming stiff-necked), so that your heart soil stays fertile for growing in friendship with Him.

3. When you wake up in the morning, invite Jesus to join you in your day, and ask Him to help you stay with Him in your heart throughout the day. Also, periodically give Jesus an extra invitation whenever you go to different places, such as to work or to eat dinner.

4. If possible, spend daily quality alone time with Jesus. Take time to read the Bible, paying close attention to those things that stand out to you, and share your heart with Him.

5. Occasionally take time to silently enjoy Jesus' presence. Take time to pour out your heart to

Jesus by sharing with Him your deepest heart's desires and concerns.

6. Take time to have the pond of your heart be cleansed. As I said earlier, I like to do this daily.

7. Whenever you seem to lack the desire to have Jesus first in your life, ask Him to give you the following:
   a. The ability to draw near to Him in your heart.
   b. A greater measure of love in your heart for Him.
   c. The ability to wholeheartedly follow Him.
   d. A heart that places Him first before anything else.

Summary

There is a song, sung by Jonathan Butler (on Kirk Whalum's "The Gospel According to Jazz" Chapter II CD), that has a wonderful line in it, which talks about when someone falls in love with Jesus, it's the best thing they ever did. In this chapter, we have explored some of the keys needed to grow in a deep love-friendship with Jesus, just as Mary did. If Jesus enables us to grow in these things, then it will bring only good effects to our lives.

[1]Silverwind, "By His Spirit" (The Sparrow Corporation, 1985), SPC 1096. Used by permission.

Chapter 5

A Priority of Time

When I graduated from college and entered the job market, I moved to a new city and found that my evenings were filled with lots of free time. For the next few years, I spent a great deal of time reading the Bible (paying special attention to those things that seemed to stand out to me), sharing my heart with God, and journaling my thoughts. When I look back at this time, I realize that this was when my friendship with Jesus really began to blossom.

Later on I married, bought a house, and had children, and I found that my free time shrank considerably. I didn't want to be a negligent parent, so not only did I spend a lot of time with my kids, but I would share my quality time with Jesus with my children. The "quality" aspect of this time considerably decreased and became much more sporadic. So, instead of spending one-and-a-half to two hours a day with Jesus as I had done when I was first out of college, I was only able to spend a little bit of time here and there, and rarely every day.

At first I didn't realize how having less quality time with Jesus was affecting me. But soon I began to notice that my thoughts drifted more quickly toward vacation times and retirement than they ever had before. I began to wonder, *What am I looking for in the extra time that vacation or retirement would provide? Am I missing something in my life?*

As I asked Jesus for wisdom about these questions, I eventually realized that I was missing the fullness of life that I used to have. The real problem was that my spiritual gas tank was low because I rarely "tanked up" in quality alone time with Jesus. It dawned on me that this problem would not be solved through vacation time or retirement, which was still many years away. Instead, I needed to find a way to have more quality alone time with Jesus in my daily life. It occurred to me that if I started taking thirty to forty minutes each night alone with Jesus as soon as the kids went to bed, that would be a good start. As I began to do this almost every night, I found myself starting to "tank up" again. Consistent personal time with God began to saturate my soul, and ironically I found myself improving as a parent as the level of love, patience, and care I had for my children increased. I also found that my desire for vacation times and retirement began to diminish. So, quality, personal time with Jesus began to positively

A Priority of Time

affect my marriage, my parenting, and the rest of my life, as well. It was a striking contrast to what had been occurring, and it showed me what a great need we all have for quality alone time with Jesus.

Through this experience, I learned that it is good to occasionally evaluate how I am using my time. If I am not practical in the use of my time, I can have the deep longing to grow in all the good things I have written about in this book, but yet find that they always tend to get squeezed out of my life by other things.

So if the concepts in this book, such as having good heart soil, learning from God, and growing in friendship with Jesus, have all made sense to you, and you desire to grow in these things because they are pleasing to God, are God's best for you, and are of great benefit to you, then please join me in exploring how we use our time.

In looking at this topic, my desire is not to insult your intelligence. I realize that many of the points in this chapter are straightforward common sense. At the same time, I think it is beneficial for all of us to occasionally evaluate the use of our time so that we can spend it doing those things that are God's best for us.

I realize that you may have a more difficult schedule than I have. You may have an extremely demanding job that requires many hours. You may be a single parent trying to raise kids and make ends meet, and you find yourself constantly run ragged. Whatever your situation, if you haven't done so already, you may want to ask Jesus to give you wisdom on how to have enough quality personal time with Him so that you can be "tanked up" in a way that will positively affect the entirety of your life. Please ask Jesus to cause things to stand out to you as you read this chapter, so that He can show you what would especially be of practical value to you.

Making Time

One thing I've observed about people is that they will make time for whatever they really want to do. If they love to play golf, they'll find time to get out on the greens. If they love to listen to a certain group perform, they'll find the time, energy, and finances to somehow make it to the concerts. In the same way, if someone really wants to grow in their friendship with Jesus, they'll make time to invite Him into their life and spend quality time with Him. Fortunately, if we find this desire to be lacking in us, then we can ask Jesus for a large amount of this good desire and to also open our eyes and see the true value of a quality friendship with Him.

Whose Time Is It?

As I look at how I use my time, the following question

has been very helpful: "Does my time belong to me or to Jesus?"

PAUSE POINT
How do you view your time? Do you view it as belonging to you or to Jesus?

The Bible teaches that our lives are not our own—they belong to Him. This is actually a statement of freedom, guarding us against the temptation to compartmentalize our lives into those areas that we think belong to Jesus, and the rest that we think belong to us to do with as we please. In the long run, it is much more beneficial for us to perceive our lives (including our time) as fully belonging to Jesus and to ask Him for guidance and direction in how best to use them. If we fail to do this, we may be tempted to think that we are getting away with something, but in reality, we are only negatively affecting ourselves and others.

The following verses reinforce that it is best for our time to fully belong to Jesus. When I first read these verses years ago, I struggled with them. I knew that Jesus is completely good and that if He challenges someone, it would only be because He wants what is best for them. Yet I had a hard time understanding His love in these verses.

> *When Jesus noticed how large the crowd was growing, he instructed his disciples to cross to the other side of the lake.*

Then one of the teachers of religious law said to him, "Teacher, I will follow you no matter where you go!"

But Jesus said, "Foxes have dens to live in, and birds have nests, but I, the Son of Man, have no home of my own, not even a place to lay my head."

Another of his disciples said, "Lord, first let me return home and bury my father."

But Jesus told him, "Follow me now! Let those who are spiritually dead care for their own dead" (Matthew 8:18-22, emphasis mine).

As they were walking along someone said to Jesus, "I will follow you no matter where you go."

But Jesus replied, "Foxes have dens to live in, and birds have nests, but I, the Son of Man, have no home of my own, not even a place to lay my head."

He said to another person, "Come, be my disciple."

The man agreed, but he said, "Lord, first let me return home and bury my father."

A Priority of Time

Jesus replied, "Let those who are spiritually dead care for their own dead. Your duty is to go and preach the coming of the Kingdom of God."

Another said, "Yes, Lord, I will follow you, but first let me say good-bye to my family."

But Jesus told him, "Anyone who puts a hand to the plow and then looks back is not fit for the Kingdom of God" (Luke 9:57-62, emphasis mine).

When I first read these verses, I thought, *The man just wanted to go bury his father! Why would Jesus make such a strong statement to him?* But then I wondered if the man had all his time tied up in family and social obligations and, in turn, wasn't free to do what was God's best for him to do. So, in Jesus' love for the man, He challenged him to fully give his time to God. If the man did so, I wouldn't have been surprised if later on Jesus guided him to return and help bury his relative, not out of social obligation, but with God's love flowing through him to his family.

Commitments

If this man truly had all his time tied up in family and social obligations, what commitments had he made? This is a good question to occasionally ask ourselves:

"To what have I committed my time?" Many people have a tendency to commit themselves to so many things that their lives are totally consumed with busy schedules. These people might conclude that they are doing what God wants them to do since they are keeping their time commitments, but I've seen people so busy in their schedules that they have no time at all to spend alone with Jesus.

At the beginning of a college semester, there are many things for which a student can sign up—clubs, social events, or intramural sports. But if a student signs up for too many activities, they may find little time left to study. In a similar way, if we are not over committed and we stay less busy, we will be able to spend quality alone time with Jesus, as well as do a quality job in those things to which we are committed.

It is good for us to pray for wisdom in deciding the things to which we should commit ourselves. I try to never make a commitment until I first ask Jesus for wisdom and determine that it seems like the right thing for me to do.

Leisure Time

PAUSE POINT

Please contemplate the following questions about your leisure time.
- What do you tend to do with your leisure time?

A Priority of Time

- Do you consider your leisure time to belong to you or to Jesus?
- If you do consider your leisure time to belong to Jesus, how can you best use it for His pleasure?

Because leisure time is so important to many of us, we can be easily tempted to compartmentalize it and classify it as *our time* instead of *Jesus' time*. We may not want to give our leisure time to Jesus or ask Him how best to use it. We can easily buy into the idea that we've worked hard at our jobs, our lessons, or our chores, and now we deserve to spend our time in relaxing ways.

It is easy to become "religious" about the things we do in our leisure time. We may feel that it is our right or duty to read the entire newspaper every day, play certain sports, watch certain TV shows, or do the daily crossword puzzle. We can conclude that these activities are our right and we need them to be refreshed, and we may feel bad if we cannot complete one of these activities.

It is very easy to fill up all of our leisure time with such activities and never get around to spending quality time with Jesus. A friend of mine would watch three hours of TV every night, yet found it difficult finding time to spend with Jesus.

However, if we push Jesus out of our leisure time, we will miss out on having our deepened friendship with

Him positively affect the rest of our lives. If you have done this but yet have a deep desire to grow in those things that are Jesus' best for you, then you may want to try the following: Share your heart with Jesus and commit all of your leisure time to Him, asking Him for wisdom on how best to use it. Consider spending the first part of your leisure time in quality personal time with Him. This is what my friend eventually decided to do. Rather than watching TV for three hours each night, he took the first hour and spent it with the Lord. That was all that was needed for him to finally have daily time with Jesus. He still watched some TV afterwards, but television no longer came before God.

PAUSE POINT
How do you think you can be best refreshed as a human being?

Because God knows best how we can be refreshed, it would be good for us to consider what He points us to in the Bible. My spiritual gas tank was on empty until I was finally able to establish some personal time with Jesus almost every day.

> *Let the words of Christ [Jesus], in all their richness, live in your hearts and make you wise. Use his words to teach and counsel each other. Sing psalms and hymns and spiritual songs to God with thankful hearts* (Colossians 3:16).

A Priority of Time

The first place for us to be refreshed is in our relationship with Jesus, because this is where our souls will truly be watered. Watching TV and other relaxing activities may provide us with a break from our schedules, and they may even be enjoyable, but they still do not meet the deepest needs of our souls. It is like eating junk food instead of a solid meal. Junk food is fun to eat, but it does not have the same nutritional value as a solid meal. I may not always find my time with Jesus to be refreshing as I immediately begin to read the Bible and share my heart with Him. Sometimes it is like starting a car on a cold day—it takes time for the car to warm up and run smoothly. But the more I am able to consistently take this time with Him, the more I find my heart filling up with His riches. Like money in the bank, it begins to accumulate interest.

Years ago, when I first tried to spend quiet time with Jesus, I found it difficult to keep at it. I often found myself tempted to do other things, such as fall asleep, get something to eat, watch TV, or even vacuum! But by sticking to it, I now find it to be the time in my day to which I look forward the most. What greater privilege could there be than to personally spend time with the magnificent Creator of the universe? How great it is to be with the One who loves me completely! So, if you are finding it difficult to get your spiritual "engine" started, I'd suggest you ask Jesus to help you to have rich times of fellowship with Him.

Quality Personal Time

Throughout this chapter, I have mentioned quality alone time with Jesus, but I realize that this may not always be feasible. When I have gone on some vacations with my family, we have stayed at hotels where there was only one room. At those times, my family has been with me when I take my quality time with Jesus. You may live with your family in a small house or apartment that doesn't allow you to easily find time alone with Jesus. If this is the case, perhaps you can find personal time during your lunch break at work. Whatever your situation, please do not feel that I am laying down a "law" by saying that you must have quality personal time with Jesus without others around. If you ask Him for wisdom, He will guide you into what is best for you to do. My desire is that Jesus would show each of us how best to have quality time with Him.

Practical Things We Can Do

The following is a list of practical things we can do to use our time wisely.

1. Commit all of our time to Jesus.
2. Ask Jesus for the following:
   a. Help to see our schedules as not our own, but belonging to Him, and to see how this can bring real freedom to our lives.

A Priority of Time

    b. Wisdom and guidance to use our time in a way that is pleasing to Him.
    c. Help to see where we may be unhealthily compartmentalizing our lives, or attempting to lock Him out of those compartments.
    d. Wisdom to commit to the right things.
    e. Help to consistently take time alone with Him and for that time to be truly rich and nurturing to our friendship with Him.

3. Commit all of our leisure time to Jesus, spending the first of that time in quality personal time with Him. During this time, it is good for us to read the Bible, pay special attention to those things that seem to stand out, and share our hearts with Jesus. May this, in turn, positively affect our friendship with Him, as well as the rest of our lives.

Summary

The purpose of this chapter has been to come before God and evaluate our use of time. Mary made it a priority to sit at Jesus' feet, learn from Him, and grow in her friendship with Him, despite her sister's demands to help with the meal preparations. Mary stuck by her priorities, and Jesus commended her for it. My desire is that Jesus would make us wise in the use of our time and in our priorities, and enable us to live lives that are pleasing to Him.

Chapter 6

Summary

The focus of this book has been to help us live life well at the feet of Jesus, the One who is the center of the universe, the most wonderful, excellent Being we could ever come to know. I'm thankful for the opportunity to share many key concepts to living our lives well at Jesus' feet. Hopefully you have heard what Jesus has wanted to say to you through this book, and He has given you wisdom on how best to apply these things in your life.

There is value and freedom in these key concepts:
- Daily picking up our crosses and following Jesus.
- Putting the entirety of our lives on God's altar.
- Keeping our minds and hearts cleansed, and maintaining soft and open hearts before Jesus.
- Learning from Jesus in all of life.
- Growing in close friendship with Jesus, daily inviting Him to be with us, and asking Him to help us to be with Him through the day.
- Being wise in our use of time.

Summary

If you are learning from Jesus and growing in your friendship with Him, then He will continue to bring you into His very best for your life.

Practical Things We Can Do

Before closing, I'd like to list two final practical suggestions.

1. On your own, you may want to take a final review of the sections titled "Practical Things We Can Do," found near the end of Chapters 3 through 5. Before reading these sections, please ask Jesus to give you a sense of how He thinks these things are working in your life. May He then cause things to stand out to you and give you a sense of any changes that would be good for you to make.

2. Please join me in re-reading this book every year or two, in order to keep focused on the things that will help us continue to live our lives well at Jesus' feet.

Thank you for allowing me to share my heart with you through this book. My desire for you is the same desire I have for myself—that Jesus' very best would come forth beautifully in our lives.

Appendix

Further Ideas on How to Read and Study the Bible

Earlier in this book, I suggested that we ask God to teach us in all of life and take time to read the Bible daily. As we ask God to teach us in all of life, when we read the Bible, God will most likely make certain things stand out to us. If we pause and contemplate those things, it can be amazing how God will help us to see how those things pertain to what we are currently going through in our daily lives.

If you have never read the Bible before, you may find the following reading path to be helpful. This is the path I took when I first read the Bible. If you already read the Bible, but would like a new reading path, then I welcome you to try it as well.

1. Read the book of John, and then the entire New Testament (Matthew through Revelation).

2. Read the New Testament two more times.

3. Put three bookmarks in the Bible: one in the Old Testament (Genesis through Malachi), one in the Gospels (Matthew through John), and one in the rest of the New Testament (Acts through Revelation). Each time you sit down to read, read one chapter from the

section behind each bookmark. When your bookmark hits the end of a section, just move it back to the beginning. For example, when you reach the end of the book of John, put the bookmark back at the beginning of the book of Matthew.

4. When your first bookmark reaches the end of the Old Testament book of Malachi, then either repeat step 3 or go on to step 5.

5. Put five bookmarks in the Bible: two that divide the Old Testament, one in the Gospels, and two that divide the rest of the New Testament:
- Bookmark 1   Genesis through Job
- Bookmark 2   Psalms through Malachi
- Bookmark 3   Matthew through John
- Bookmark 4   Acts through Ephesians
- Bookmark 5   Philippians through Revelation

Each time you sit down to read, read one chapter from the sections behind bookmarks 1, 3, and 4. The next time you read, read from the sections behind bookmarks 2, 3, and 5. When bookmark 1 gets to the end of Job, wait until bookmark 2 gets to the end of Malachi. Then move both bookmarks 1 and 2 to their beginning points of Genesis and Psalms (since you have just completed reading the Old Testament). When bookmark 3 gets to the end of John, move it to the beginning of Matthew (since you have just completed reading the Gospels). When bookmark 4 gets to the end of Ephesians, wait until bookmark 5 gets to the end of Revelation. Then move both bookmarks 4 and 5 to their beginning points of Acts and Philippians (since you have just completed reading the New Testament).

6. Try other things, such as reading different Bible translations or moving your bookmarks in different ways. For example, you could read an entire book of the Bible at one bookmark before moving to read an entire book at your next bookmark, and so forth.

I have found this reading path to be of real value to me, and I truly believe that God directed me to read His Word in this way. After reading through the Bible many times, I realize some of the reasons why.

If I simply open the Bible and read on whatever page it opens to, I have occasionally found a verse or passage that has been just what I needed at that point in time. But if this is my only way of reading the Bible, it would be difficult for me to gain a fuller understanding of the entire Bible. It is like reading any book: I may want to skim the book or read the summary before reading it from cover to cover. But if all I do is skim the book or read the summary, I will never gain a full understanding of the book. It would also make it more difficult to consistently read the book, because I will never know when I have completed it. Having a reading path that takes me through the whole Bible has helped me to stay consistent in reading it almost every day.

The Gospels (Matthew, Mark, Luke, and John) focus

especially on Jesus. And because Jesus is God, watching Him interact with others will give us insight into how God interacts with people, including showing us what He likes and dislikes. The reading path I have provided begins with the Gospels and places the heaviest concentration of reading on them.

Many things in the Old Testament (Genesis through Malachi) make sense in light of the New Testament (Matthew through Revelation), so I'm glad I read the New Testament a few times before I started to read the Old Testament. Also, when using the three or five bookmark system, I wind up with a greater concentration of reading in the New Testament than in the Old Testament.

Lastly, one reason I suggest to eventually place bookmarks at different places in the Bible is that different parts of the Bible have different focuses. It's like a meal that consists of different foods, such as meat, potatoes, salad, vegetables, bread, and dessert. I like to "eat" from different areas of the Bible for a varied and well-balanced spiritual diet. If a chapter at one bookmark seems a little dry, often sections at the other bookmarks wind up being quite tasty.

ABOUT THE AUTHOR

Scott Brooks lived the first 19 years of his life as an atheist. During his college years, he asked that if God were really there (which Scott didn't think was the case), He would make himself known to him. Scott was amazed to not only learn that God actually exists, but that God also desires to have a close friendship with each of us. After joining a Bible study and learning about Jesus' payment on the cross and resurrection, Scott decided to commit his life to God, receive Jesus' payment on the cross, and enter into a friendship with God.

Being amazed that there was so much more to life than he originally thought, Scott began to wonder what else he had misjudged in his atheist years. Knowing that God had the answers, Scott began to periodically ask God to teach him through all of life (including what he was reading in the Bible) and to help him to understand truth about Himself and reality. This path of learning eventually led to the writing of *At His Feet*, which contains many practical how-to concepts for life.

By trade Scott has been a computer programmer for more than 20 years. He lives in south central Pennsylvania with his wife and two children.

TO CONTACT THE AUTHOR
FOR SPEAKING ENGAGEMENTS:

Go to www.ScottRBrooks.com and click on "Contact" to get the most up-to-date information on how to get in contact with Scott.

www.ingramcontent.com/pod-product-compliance
Lightning Source LLC
Chambersburg PA
CBHW052056070526
44584CB00017B/2211